The Trinity in the Gospel of John

The Trinity
in the
Gospel
of John

A Thematic Commentary on the Fourth Gospel

Royce Gordon Gruenler

BAKER BOOK HOUSE
Grand Rapids, Michigan 49506

ISBN: 0-8010-3806-5

Library of Congress Catalog Card Number: 85-62745

Printed in the United States of America

Contents

Preface

The discourses of Jesus in the Gospel of John have long held a fascination for me, as they have for other interpreters of the fourth Gospel. After a long flirtation with process theology that endured during the 1960s and ended in the early 1970s, I returned to the centrality of the Word as the focus of my exegetical and theological studies, but not without a sense of the social nature of God that is vital to the process school as well as to biblical revelation. But where God is seen in unitarian terms by most process people and is thought to be dependent upon us and our universe for his social experience, I came to see with a new appreciation how impressive is the biblical disclosure of God's Triunity and the revelation that God as Father, Son, and Holy Spirit is essentially social and inexhaustibly dynamic quite apart from the created world. Scripture implies that God is the divine Community who is at once one and plural in everlasting love and fellowship. It is this Triune Society of divine persons in absolute unity that is original and archetypal and leaves its stamp of dynamic oneness and plurality on everything that is created. Family, social, and communitarian language is accordingly evident throughout Scripture and appears as an essential component of creation itself and as the central theme of redemptive history. One can trace intimations of the family and social Trinity motif in the writings of some of the great figures of Christian thought, from the Cappadocians Gregory of Nazianzus and Gregory of Nyssa to Richard of Saint Victor, John Calvin, Jonathan Edwards, and B. B. Warfield, but in none, surprisingly, is the theme developed as fully and exegetically as one would wish in view of the witness of Scripture, especially the fourth Gospel.

No single biblical book speaks more to this theme of God's fundamentally social nature than does the Gospel of John. I had originally conceived an exegetical study of the Trinity in the New Testament and in the Old, and its implications for Christian ethics, as a project of a single book. As it turned out, the Gospel of John is too rich fare for such slight treatment and demanded a whole volume of its own. This is what I now present to the reader, in expectation that two other studies on the Trinity will appear in future to give account of the divine Community in the remainder of Scripture as well as its application to Christian life and thought.

Readers who might be disappointed that I have not concentrated on Paul or Hebrews or other important biblical sources will accordingly understand that the present study focuses principally on an exegesis of John and that the second volume will examine and exegete the remaining New Testament material on the Trinity, together with Old Testament intimations. This book with its sequels is designed in style and format for a wide audience because I feel the subject to be of such importance. I have purposely avoided a "garland of ibids," although I have continually interacted with scholarly literature on the subject, in order that the major themes of Jesus and the Trinity in the Gospel of John may be presented as clearly and as simply as possible, without encumbrance. Lay readers and students should find it not too hard to read and, I hope, compelling in argument, although a few terms (e.g., "disposability"—availability to others) will take getting used to, while professional scholars in biblical studies and theology will recognize a serious grappling with large issues which (again I hope) will advance in some measure our understanding of the nature of God's social activity as it is described in the fourth Gospel.

As I indicate in the opening chapter and concluding Appendix, I have attempted to be primarily exegetical in listening to the discourses of Jesus in John and drawing forth the disclosures of God's social nature in the activity of the incarnate Son. This method requires a running commentary on the text of John and the testing of the theme of God's social nature that has been discerned through prior reflection on the Gospel. Scientific method in the exegetical process, as in any scientific undertaking, requires a careful examination of data in view of a hypothesis that the exegete seeks to confirm or disprove by testing.

Although in some critical circles considerable skepticism hangs over the Gospel as far as the historical reliability of the discourses of Jesus is concerned, especially those in which he makes high christological claims of oneness with the Father, I have avoided the attempt to distinguish so-called authentic or historical sayings from those supposed by a number of critics to have been created by the evangelist and placed on Jesus' lips.

This issue I have discussed at some length in the Appendix. Suffice it here to say that the question cannot be resolved neutrally by appeal to the scientific tools of exegesis, for exegetical tools are employed according to the presuppositions of the exegete, principal among them the christological question of whether one can really bring oneself to believe that the Son of God could take on human flesh and speak in the manner of the Jesus of the fourth Gospel. If one cannot believe that, then the tools of exegesis will be used to explain the "high" sayings of Jesus as pious reflections of the evangelist and his tradition which have been placed on the lips of Jesus after the fact. The sayings in question will then be of uncertain value in determining the real nature of God as Triune Family, except perhaps in some symbolic or docetic sense that substantially diminishes the importance of the historical incarnation of the Son and accordingly the genuine manifestation of the social Trinity in the redemptive process within time and space.

I recognize that there are neoorthodox and even some evangelical scholars who take the more skeptical view that Jesus was not conscious of his eternal relationship with the divine Triunity and that his utterances to the contrary in the fourth Gospel are actually theological reflections of later redactors and editors, possibly relying on inspired Christian prophets. Although I was once sympathetic to this point of view I have been disappointed by the lack of solid evidence for the existence of such prophets and their widespread creation of new sayings of Jesus in the redactional process. Of even greater weight is the fact that the view is not really in harmony with the strongly incarnational theme of the Gospel. For if one considers the evangelist a fellow believer in the community of faith which the Son, together with the Father and the Spirit, brought into being, then it is not only possible but also (I believe) more historically and exegetically proper to say that the discourses of Jesus in John bear faithful witness to Jesus the incarnate Son and his conscious disclosure of the intention of the Triune Community to create a new community of believers.

Not only did the disclosure of God's dynamic social nature appear in a new light during the process of exegeting the discourses of Jesus, but also there appeared something quite remarkable about the attitude of the persons of the Triune Community that I now see to be deeply characteristic of God as well as of the society of believers when it truly reflects the Triune Society. It is what I have called (following Gabriel Marcel) the attribute of disposability, that is, of being there for the other as servants who place themselves at the other person's disposal in an act of hospitality and generosity. The servant theme of disposability runs deep in both Old and New Testaments and is particularly strong in the Gospel of John. In Jesus the incarnate Lord irony is personified, for his authority as Lord is expressed in quite the opposite way one would expect from one of his stature and divine origin. The Word who is with God and is God takes on human flesh and becomes a servant by placing himself at the disposal of a lost world. This irony of the unexpected is a key that unlocks many rooms in the Gospel that beg to be entered.

To an eminent degree in the fourth Gospel the attribute of disposability characterizes not only the attitude of the Son and the Holy Spirit, as we would expect, but the Father as well, without diminishing his formal authority as Father. We are not accustomed to think of the Father as servant, but I will leave it to the reader to decide whether careful attention to the discourses of Jesus in John does not reveal an ironic biblical truth about personhood, beginning with the original persons of the Triune Community, namely, that one is truly a Self or a self not only in making claims of individuality and authority (as Father and Son do explicitly and the

Spirit does implicitly) but even more so in manifesting a love that rejoices in serving and pleasing the other. Juxtaposed in Jesus' discourses are two kinds of statements: those that express his coequality with the Father and those that express his faithful servanthood on the Father's behalf. Similarly, while the Father is given pride of place by the Son, he is seen to defer to the Son by honoring and glorifying him as appointed spokesman on behalf of the divine Family, and by faithfully listening and responding to the Son's requests on behalf of himself and the community of believers.

Father and Son similarly (the text implies) honor the Holy Spirit as appointed spokesman and interpreter in the present age, while the Holy Spirit (again implied) reciprocally honors and serves the Father and the Son. Moreover, the three persons of the Triune Family not only serve one another but also are seen, remarkably, to be servants of a fallen race as they perform the ultimate act of disposability in the willing gift of the Son upon the cross. Finally, in the Johannine eschatology of envelopment as the family circle widens, the redeemed disciples are invited to wash one another's feet as servants to the world and feed the Lord's sheep in continuing acts of hospitality and disposability, for they have been adopted into the wider circle of the divine Family as children. This is stated thematically at the beginning of the Gospel: "But to all who received him, who believed in his name, he gave power to become children of God; who were born, not of blood nor of the will of the flesh nor of the will of man, but of God" (1:12–13).

The implications of the social nature of God and the attributes of disposability and generosity are considerable for further exegesis of Scripture, especially the synoptic Gospels and the Epistles, and for a sharper perception of the ethical mandate of the believing community, not to mention a more comprehensive Christian view of the extended families of creation and their interrelation, all the way from the atomic to the human families of earth. I have touched only briefly on these matters in the present book, and they invite further study (the third volume in the trilogy will examine exegetically the biblical teaching on "The Trinity in Church and World"). At the very least the present volume partially fulfills an agenda expressed in the closing pages of my critique of process theism (*The Inexhaustible God: Biblical Faith and the Challenge of Process Theism* [Grand Rapids: Baker, 1983], p. 201) where I noted a need "to pay careful attention to the biblical grounds for trinitarian theology, making clear that in his own personal and infinite being God supremely exemplifies both unity and diversity as First Family and at the same time supremely exemplifies steadfastness of character and inexhaustible, dynamic love as Father, Son, and Holy Spirit." It is my hope that this exegetical study of Jesus' discourses in the Gospel of John will provide fresh insights and a new appreciation of the social nature and generosity of the Triune God, especially as God's awesome authority is expressed through the Son in ironic love and disposability on behalf of a sinful world.

I wish to express thanks to my colleagues in Biblical Studies and Theology at Gordon-Conwell Theological Seminary (especially Greg Beale, David Gordon, Philip Payne, Roger Nicole, and David Wells, among others) who encouraged the project and at various points discussed important issues relating to the study and made helpful criticisms and suggestions. Thanks are due also the faculty senate, administration, and trustees of the Seminary who granted me a half-year sabbatical to complete the manuscript. I am also grateful to members of the Boston Theological Society who critiqued my introductory chapter from a variety of theological positions and helped me tighten my defense against possible charges of Apollinarianism and tritheism. My response has been to claim good company in the apostle John, whose Gospel bears witness to the full incarnation of the Son, and whose insistence on the unity of the persons of the divine Community guards against the danger of tritheism. It is enlightening, if not enheartening, to discover how widely in contemporary theology the language of classical trinitarianism is used in a modal or functional manner that operates out of a basic unitarianism (i.e., God appears to function in the world as Father, as Son, as Spirit, but is not really internally social as the Triune God). That presupposition is not only speculative and fails to do justice to Johannine language, but also affords no essential insight into the social nature of God and creation, except perhaps along the lines of process theism where the social universe is necessary to an otherwise abstract and lonely deity.

I wish to express my appreciation to those who critiqued the completed manuscript and who, while agreeing supportively with my interpretation of the social nature of the Trinity and the need for a greater emphasis on servanthood in the exercise of authority, made a number of suggestions for correcting and improving the argument. I have incorporated many of those suggestions in the final revision. One reader has argued that distinction in roles, where one gives an order and another obeys, does not necessarily entail the conclusion that one is superior or inferior to another, and that self-sacrificing notions (such as disposability) must not be allowed to slur over distinctions in authority/submission relationships that are taught in Scripture and need to be observed in the order of Father, Son, and Holy Spirit, as well as in the divinely established orders of authority in church and society. I have tried to take this caveat into account in the remarks that follow and hope that my thematic emphasis on mutual servanthood will not be misconstrued as an egalitarian attack on levels of authority that are biblically described and mandated.

At the same time I express concern that overemphasizing the model of authority/submission may reintroduce the one-way subordinationism that troubled earlier discussion of the Trinity in the history of the church. If one wishes to say, using the language of Jesus in the fourth Gospel, that within the inner relationship of the eternal Triunity the Father always commands and the Son and Spirit always obey, that only the Father authoritatively speaks and the Son and Spirit always passively listen, but never the other way around, and that yet at the same time neither is principally inferior or superior to the other, then language has failed me at some point, for a category mistake would seem to have slipped into the argument that does not carefully distinguish when the proposition might be true and when it should be deemed false. The best one could do under these circumstances to salvage Jesus' claims of equality with the Father would be to speak of this equality on the impersonal level of unity of substance in the Trinity (category 1) where there is perfect oneness, coupled however with inequality on the level of subsistence as intercommuning persons (category 2). At least one discussant actually takes this point of view and argues that the Son is absolutely one with the Father only on the level of undifferentiated substance or essence, while in their actual personal relationship as Father and Son (the Spirit being a subordinate third party) they are unequal, because the Son and Spirit are eternally subordinate to the Father. The Father always commands, the Son and Spirit always listen and obey.

I question whether Jesus had such subtleties in mind when he said, "Before Abraham was, I am" (8:58); "I and the Father are one" (10:30); "I am in the Father and the Father in me" (14:11); "All that the Father has is mine" (16:15). It is important to note the personal genre of Jesus' address when he uses the personal pronoun *I* and the personal proper noun *Father* in these claims. Jesus is not talking about impersonal substance; he does not mean to say that as Son he is actually unequal to the Father as far as their personal relationship is concerned, while one with the Father only on the level of their common substance. The question cannot be resolved in that direction. If the language of Jesus is to be exegeted properly as the expression of his relationship to the Father then it must be recognized that his statements of subordination (he is sent, he listens, he obeys) are the language of the incarnate Son who has voluntarily assumed a subordinate role in time and space for the work of salvation. The subordination of Son and Spirit to the Father is for the time of redemption only; hence Jesus' subordinationist language describes what have traditionally been called the "modes of operation" that pertain to the accomplishment of the redemptive task. Jesus' claims to coequality with the Father constitute on the other hand what theologians have technically termed "modes of subsistence" and describe the necessary relation of the persons of the Trinity.

The two-categories solution is somewhat reminiscent of the price the Cappadocian Fathers paid for their (correct) insistence on the three personalities and their (incorrect) definition of their unity as abstract, impersonal essence, thus sacrificing the idea of the personal God. On the testimony of the fourth Gospel it is clear to me that unity and coequality are integral to the personal interaction of Father and Son (and by implication, of the Spirit), and that even the apparent subordinationist language of Jesus can be seen ironically to attest a characteristic attitude of mutual disposability and deference that flows from unity with the Father.

But there is another problem in literally extrapolating into the interrelationship of the eternal divine Family Jesus' language about always listening to and obeying the Father and being less than the Father. It would mean that only the Father would have authority to speak, while the Son (and Spirit) would be eternally cast in the role of passive listeners. That is of course absurd and no one would go so far as to follow it to such a logical conclusion. Yet that is what must logically follow if the sent/listen/obey sayings of Jesus are taken as absolutes that describe the eternal relationship of Son (and Spirit) to the Father. Rather, as I have argued in the study, they are to be exegeted as a genre of language by which Jesus dramatically and ironically describes his voluntary servanthood on behalf of the divine Family in the redemptive program. That this is so should be clear from his alternating-equality statements, as well as his discourses with the Father where the Father listens and (so the texts imply) does the bidding of the Son.

Perhaps the problem arises only when one begins with a hermeneutical principle derived from New Testament texts on headship (1 Cor. 11; Eph. 5) which are interpreted to mean that on the personal level the husband commands (lovingly) and the wife obeys (respectfully), but never the other way around, while on the spiritual level (corresponding perhaps to the substance of the Trinity) all differences are transcended ("there is neither male nor female; for you are all one in Christ Jesus," Gal. 3:28). It is not my purpose in this book to argue the cogency or inadequacy of that interpretation of the headship of husband over wife, but I would suggest that it is logically difficult to hold to a command/obey relationship on the one hand and on the other to deny that in some important sense one party is superior and the other inferior. That may very well be true and necessary in view of the presence of sin in the present age. But when applied to the Trinity that principle lands one flatly in subordinationism in respect to the interpersonal relationship of Son and Spirit to the Father who must perforce be seen as the superior member of the Triune Family. In the Gospel of John Jesus does indeed listen to and obey the Father, but if we look carefully at the text as a whole we will see that the Father also exhibits the "modes of operation" as he listens to the Son, grants his requests, bears witness to him, and glorifies him (8:18, 50, 54; 12:28; 14:16, 26; 15:26; 16:13–15; 17:1, 5) in a mutuality that is underscored by Jesus' claims to absolute coequality with the Father (10:30; 14:9, 11; 17:11, 21). This is what makes Jesus' language in the Gospel so remarkable and so ironic.

I should alert the reader that I have not tampered with the Father/Son language in the Gospel of John or addressed those who wish to feminize divine titles and pronouns. That issue goes beyond my simple agenda of interpreting the social nature and hospitality of the Triune Community in John. Suffice it to say that I am aware, as any interpreter should be, that Jesus' use of ordinary language and his heightening of relational models drawn from common relationships (e.g., fathers and sons) indicates that the original Father/Son relationship is far richer than the pale replica that is seen in this bent creation. Family images also (and my term *the Triune Family*) must be seen as humble pointers to the unimaginably richer and absolutely original relationship of Father, Son, and Holy Spirit. Yet they are legitimate models because God has created the world in his social image, making it possible for the incarnate Son to use our language and lift it upward toward its origin, himself embodying in his person as God-man (in what has been called the enhypostatic union of humanity and divine Word) the perfect image of the original relationship.

The theme of mutual and voluntary subordination among the persons of the Triune Family counters the notion that there is an essential or necessary inequality among the persons of the Trinity (the subordinationist error that Calvin laid to rest by his exegetically sound insistence on the absolute coequality of Father, Son, and Holy Spirit, a position biblically documented at length by Warfield in his essay, "The Biblical Doctrine of the Trinity," one of the finest studies on the Trinity ever written. See his *Biblical and Theological Studies*, ed. Samuel G. Craig [Philadelphia: Presbyterian and Reformed, 1952], pp. 22–59). The Gospel of John intimates that each of the persons of the Triunity willingly, lovingly, and voluntarily seeks to serve and please the other. This does not diminish the distinctive roles of Father, Son, and Holy Spirit, but highlights their co-inherence as interacting persons (traditionally termed *perichoresis* and *circumincessio* = mutual containment, interpenetration, and indwelling). Our study describes one of the characteristic modes by which the persons of the Triune Family disclose their interaction in the redemptive process. The incarnate Son subordinates himself to the will of the Father for the work of salvation, and the Holy Spirit subordinates himself to the will of Father and Son in carrying out the work. (It is important to note that the self-disclosure of the Trinity is incidental to though it accompanies the accomplishment of redemption). But it is also clear from Jesus' complementary claims to equality with the Father (10:30; 17:11) and his intimation that the Holy Spirit shares equally in carrying out the work of salvation (14:16–17, 26; 16:13–15) that such subordination is voluntarily assumed and flows out of the dynamic and mutual hospitality of the divine Family as a unity.

The interpreter must be alert at this point to analyze all the data carefully and observe that there are sufficient clues in the Gospel of John to allow us to speak of a subordination within the Trinity that is mutual, voluntary, and loving, but not of a subordination in which the Son and Holy Spirit are second- and third-class members of the Family. Jesus' claims to equality with the Father should make it clear that his subordination as incarnate Son is voluntarily assumed for the work of redemption, and that this voluntary sense may be extrapolated to the equally subordinate role of the Holy Spirit in the redemptive process.

We are popularly accustomed to think of the Trinity in a descending order of authority, Father first, Son second, Holy

Spirit third because we refer to them in that accustomed order (Jesus deferentially uses that order in Matt. 28:19). But that may be understood as a convention of speech which describes the modes of operation in the redemptive process, flowing from a mutual and voluntary agreement between Father, Son, and Holy Spirit. How could it be otherwise if they are truly united in will and purpose, as Jesus asserts so often in the Gospel? He can say that he is sent by the Father and that he listens to the Father, but that suggests an essential and necessary subordination only if he has to be sent and has to listen because otherwise he would not wish to go or hear what the Father has to say. On the contrary, sending and listening have just the opposite connotation in the Gospel, again ironic, for the text implies that Jesus is sent because he wants to be sent, and listens because he already is in full accord with the divine intention to redeem a fallen world.

One of my colleagues has observed that there is after all no eternal Father without an eternal Son, just as there is no eternal Son without an eternal Father. Father and Son should not therefore imply relations of first and second class, or any temporal ordering. We may also assume from the witness of John that there is no Father or Son without a Holy Spirit and no Holy Spirit without a Son or a Father, certainly not in the modes of redemptive operation, for the work of salvation is incomplete without the ministry of the Spirit. Moreover, when Scripture refers to the divine persons the order can be interchanged (2 Cor. 13:14); the order can be reversed (1 Cor. 12:4–6; Eph. 4:4–6); just as pride of place can be accorded the generative activity of the Holy Spirit in the Son's incarnation (Luke 1:35; Matt. 1:20).

Accordingly one must not mistake voluntary submission for necessary submission, for the latter will regress inevitably to a one-way subordination of Son and Spirit to the Father (and may lead in the end to Arianism). It would not be good exegesis to reintroduce such subordinationism into the Trinity in order to sanction unequal roles of authority and obedience within the believing community. Unequal roles are often required in church and society to check the presence of selfishness and evil that are the effects of the fall,

but in the age to come even marriage itself will be super-
seded by some unimaginably higher relationship (Matt.
22:30).

Indeed, the fourth Gospel (in concert with the Synoptics)
announces that the eschatological age to come has already
been inaugurated in the person and ministry of Jesus and
invites a kind of mutuality and disposability that images the
Triune Society itself. One notes that Jesus speaks with awesome judgmental authority mainly where his generous hospitality on behalf of the divine Family is willfully rejected,
where unbelievers refuse the invitation to come home and
willfully choose death instead of life by seeking self-actualization on their own rebellious and selfish terms. But where
believers respond to Jesus' invitation they become like him
and exercise authority principally by becoming servants in a
manner that mirrors his own servant lordship.

I hope that the theme of mutual disposability, one of the
central themes of this study on the fourth Gospel, will be
found to be applicable by the majority of the readers of this
book, and that all of us may prove in the truest sense to be
servants of one another as we reflect upon the generous hospitality of the First Family. Though there is an extensive
literature on the issue of the role of men and women within
the believing family which seems to focus largely on the
proper exegesis of a strategic group of texts (principally 1
Cor. 11:3–15; 14:33–35; Eph. 5:21–33; 1 Tim. 2:8–15), I
would hope that John's emphasis on the disposability and
servanthood of Jesus the Son in our behalf might provide a
larger context for exegesis of these and related passages and
engender at the very least a responsive attitude of disposability and servanthood toward one another, regardless of
role or rank, as Jesus exemplifies in the footwashing of his
disciples when he says, "For I have given you an example,
that you also should do as I have done to you. Truly, truly, I
say to you, a servant is not greater than his master; nor is he
who is sent greater than he who sent him" (13:15–16). As
humble hospitality characterizes the Son, so, says our Lord,
should it characterize the believer.

Yet even that is not Jesus' last word on the subject, for in
the context of loving disposability (15:12–17) a higher rela-

tionship is revealed as believers are drawn into the circle of mutual friendship with the divine Family: "No longer do I call you servants, for the servant does not know what his master is doing; but I have called you friends, for all that I have heard from my Father I have made known to you" (v. 15). This does not erase all distinctions between Jesus and his followers or diminish his lordship over them, nor does it eliminate roles of responsibility within the believing community, but it lifts all relationships to a higher family level where mutual service takes precedence over any hierarchical model of simple command/obedience.

Thus while readers of this book will undoubtedly align themselves differently on the currently warm issue of the role of men and women in teaching and ministry and on distinctions in authority/submission relationships (my closest friends and colleagues are not all agreed on the subject), none of us should gainsay the evidence of the fourth Gospel that Jesus exercises his authority not only as the Lord who judges the unbelieving but also as generous Lord and source of life for those who believe, as he savingly places himself at their disposal. He personifies servanthood and hospitality par excellence for a lost world and shows his followers how to carry that good news of salvation to those who are yet to believe. The theologian would refer to this as "exemplarist soteriology." Although each person in the community of believers is assigned by the Lord a different role of authority and responsibility, these roles are not essentially defined as opportunities for exercising hierarchical power over others (the worldly pattern), but as opportunities for responsible servanthood, where the greater the responsibility the more the servant is to be at the disposal of others (so also Mark 9:35).

In light of the Johannine revelation, one finds maximum disposability between Father, Son, and Holy Spirit in the inexhaustibly dynamic fellowship of the divine Triunity. Ideally the beloved community, in mirroring the Triune Community, is to exercise its authority on various levels not by dominating but by taking the lead in serving. Herein lies the great irony of creative power and authority in biblical terms. In the end, considering Jesus' teaching and exemplary behavior, it is not so much the fact that we exercise authority but how we fulfill our distinctive roles in creative and redemptive behavior that seems to count most in the fourth Gospel. Jesus' own exemplary activity as both Lord and Servant personifies the great New Testament principle of union in subordination.

In this vein I wish to acknowledge the contribution of my M.Div. students at Gordon-Conwell in courses on the Gospel of John, and two classes of D.Min. candidates whom it was my pleasure to teach in successive summers and who read the manuscript in its early phases and interacted creatively with the theme of "The Family in the New Testament," focused on the Triune Family in John.

I also express deep thanks to my wife and family for their generosity in providing a happy home in which to compose and write, and who, not least among their many kindnesses during the writing of this book, allowed a temporary skewing of the family finances to purchase a portable secretarial staff in the shape of a Kaypro computer and Hewlett-Packard ThinkJet printer. This electronic digital staff has been invaluable during the months of research, composition, and revision. Needless to say, for all exegetical and theological errors, I claim personal responsibility. Finally, thanks are due my Byington Fellow, Susan Choo, who has scrutinized the copy for errors and compiled the indexes; Allan Fisher for his warm encouragement and wise suggestions as editor; Sharon Zinger for her good work as editorial assistant; and Linda Triemstra, project editor, who has now, with the others, worked with me on three publications by Baker Book House.

1

The Social Nature of God

One of the compelling characteristics of God as he reveals himself in Scripture is that he speaks, converses, and is eminently social. He calls the world into being and addresses its creatures with words of exhortation, judgment, and grace, inviting the human family back to a fellowship that has been lost and to adoption into his divine community.

It is the Community of God that begs our attention in this study. The social nature of God is a theme that has often been neglected, though it is central to the redemptive story of the Bible. Surprisingly, the history of biblical interpretation and theology has seldom taken note of the fact that the Triune God is a divine Community, the Triune Society. In the fourth Gospel, which will be our focus in this book (the first of a projected trilogy on the divine Community in the New Testament), the Father and the Son are seen to be conversing within the divine Household, Father, Son, and Holy Spirit interweaving their distinctive patterns of personhood within an essential unity, and (equally important in our discussion) displaying a characteristic attitude of love and interpersonal communion as servants of one another, always glorifying and deferring to one another.

This remarkable fact, which emerges from a close examination of Jesus' dialogues with the Father in the fourth Gospel, describes a God who converses internally as a dynamic and inexhaustible divine Society. This portrait of the social God also unveils the essentially social character of the creation God has made and explains why New Testament ethics, and biblical ethics as a whole, exhorts the society of the faithful to become servants of God and of one another, and thereby to place themselves at the disposal of God and the world. Hospitality and being there for the other are, according to the Gospel of John, distinctively characteristic of the persons of the Triune Family in their relationship to each other within the essential unity that constitutes them as one God.

Clearly the implications of the social God who converses within his own Household range wide when it comes to the question of what proper Christian response in worship, service, and learning ought to be. The ethical exhortations in Old and New Testaments appear to be designed to help the believing community image the pattern of God's social nature in a common life of generosity and hospitality. Such patterning consists primarily of creative fidelity in conversation with God and one another and of being at God's disposal as faithful servants in the world. That is how Jesus summarizes the intent of the law and the commandments, as vertical service to the Lord and horizontal service to neighbor (John 13:12–17; 15:1–17; Luke 10:27). In the fourth Gospel the larger dimensions of this fidelity are clearly manifest as they reflect the fidelity of Father, Son, and Holy Spirit toward one another and toward the new society they are bringing into being, as together they draw the faithful hospitably into their inner Family circle (John 16:13–15; 17:13–26).

In the fourth Gospel true discipleship is determined by faithful response in these two dimensions. The followers of Jesus place themselves at the disposal of the Triune Community and reflect the image of the God who is essentially social and faithful to his word. The disciples become genuinely personal and communal creatures by obedient response to Jesus who, as Son of God, discloses the personal and communal nature of the divine Triunity. The Gospel of John provides the original pattern for the new community of disciples to follow by describing the social nature of God as divine Community. This is true not only of John but also is implicit in all Scripture, which attests the social nature of God and creation in biblical exhortations to love and serve God and neighbor.

In the larger view of Scripture God is heard to converse not only with his people but also within himself as divine Society. God's reality is seen to be social as it imprints its signature of unity in variety and variety in unity upon all levels of creation. All of creation, but especially its highest human level, appears designed of God to serve other levels

2

and members of the larger family of creation, and to be interdependent in some way that is analogous to the pattern by which Father, Son, and Holy Spirit are interdependent and are at one another's disposal in the most original Household, the Triune Family.

This central claim about the social nature of God is not arrived at by speculative philosophical conjecture but respects the integrity of the self-disclosure of God in Scripture. Accordingly, this study of the divine Community in the fourth Gospel is primarily exegetical and focuses on the unveiling in Scripture of the social nature of God and the created world. I have dealt critically with speculative approaches, in particular with the conjectures of process theology, in *The Inexhaustible God: Biblical Faith and the Challenge of Process Theism* (Grand Rapids: Baker, 1983), and with critical questions regarding the historical integrity of Jesus and the gospel accounts in *New Approaches to Jesus and the Gospels: A Phenomenological and Exegetical Study of Synoptic Christology* (Grand Rapids: Baker, 1982), to which the reader who desires technical foundations for the present study is directed. An Appendix is included in the present volume on the fourth Gospel; in it I present my technical reasons for accepting the historical integrity of the discourses and actions of Jesus, in contrast to the widely held opinion in critical circles that the Gospel is a mixture of historical fact and liturgical fiction. My critical observations on authorship, setting, and date are designed for those who might wonder why anyone would still consider the language of Jesus in John, especially his dialogues with the Father, to be other than later unhistorical reflections of the worshiping church. Other and more conservative readers of the book would not have thought to question the historical reliability of the conversing Jesus in John, since the Gospel portrays him as the incarnate Son of God ("And the Word became flesh," John 1:14) and validates his historical integrity through the authenticating witness of the Holy Spirit, who preserves the testimony of eyewitnesses (14:26; 17:8; 21:24).

I have tried throughout the study to be descriptive of the Gospel as it stands in its final form, without losing concentration on the narrative line by entertaining hypothetical ques-

3

tions or traversing redactional byways. My concern continually has been to enter into the mind of the evangelist and into the heart of his account, and thus (I am convinced) into the mind and intention of Jesus as the evangelist portrays him. One theme that is common to my two prior studies and the present one is that no deep insight into Jesus and the Gospels and the nature of God is to be gained when one approaches them as problems, a point well made some years ago by Gabriel Marcel (see my chapter on Marcel in *New Approaches to Jesus and the Gospels*, pp. 190–203). Problem-centered studies usually begin and end with questioners speaking in a circle to themselves, permitting texts to respond only to a set of questions asked, rather than allowing the authors through their texts to address the reader with new, and often personally disturbing, questions.

The model of exegesis I have tried to follow in this study is descriptive (and in that sense phenomenological). I have tried to be open to the phenomenon of Jesus' speaking and acting by entering into the story and suspending disbelief, asking critical questions only after being addressed (at which point the critical questions were often quite different). This attitude toward the exegetical task is a positive one of entering the Gospel of John with expectancy and belief rather than doubt and disbelief, listening openly to the discourses and conversations of Jesus and observing his actions, and placing oneself at the disposal of the word that is spoken and to the person who is speaking, as one would enter an arresting and compelling story with a certain kind of obedience and sense of being spellbound.

This approach makes a good deal of difference as to what one hears and sees and finally comes to understand about the person who is speaking, since it discloses the world in which he functions. In this case it is Jesus' world of relationships and associations. It is personally revealed by Jesus, by way of the evangelist, and is personally appropriated by the reader. Michael Polanyi has aptly made this point in describing the personal component in the process of all human knowing (*Personal Knowledge: Towards a Post-Critical Philosophy* [New York: Harper and Row, 1964]; see my discussion of Polanyi in *New Approaches*, passim). Knowing is personal knowing within a social context. In the fourth Gospel it is the personal and social God who is revealing himself to creatures who are also personal and social because they have been made in the image of the divine Community.

What is arresting as one listens to Jesus speaking in the dialogues of John is how much he reveals about the inner social relationships of God as Father, Son, and Spirit and of their oneness-in-threeness and threeness-in-oneness. Jesus does not speak of himself as less than equal with God and claims essential unity with Father and Spirit, avoiding any suggestion of tritheism (there is one God, not three). At the same time he preserves the integrity of each of the persons of the divine Community (the one God is three persons in interpersonal communion). Jesus also speaks side by side of his social equality and oneness in the divine Fellowship and of his servanthood and deference to the other persons of the Triune Family, exhibiting the original hospitality that characterizes the inner relationship of Father, Son, and Holy Spirit as divine Community.

In *The Inexhaustible God* I concluded my critique of process theism (which is long on philosophical speculation about the social nature of reality but short on biblical exegesis) with an appeal that we reexamine the biblical basis of belief in the social God who discloses himself in Scripture as the Triune Community. Several studies have appeared in recent years that have sought to articulate this important teaching in Scripture that the nature of God is essentially social. The following studies are to one degree or another worthy of note: Leonard Hodgson, *The Doctrine of the Trinity* (London: Nisbet, 1943); Arthur W. Wainwright, *The Trinity in the New Testament* (London: SPCK, 1962); a trilogy on Christology by Jean Galot, *La Personne du Christ; La Conscience de Jésus; Vers une nouvelle christologie* (Paris: Lethielleux, 1969, 1971); E. L. Mascall, *Theology and the Gospel of Christ* (London: SPCK, 1977); Bertrand de Margerie, *The Christian Trinity in History*, translated by E. J. Fortman (Still River, Mass.: Saint Bede's Publications, 1982); Jürgen Moltmann, *The Trinity and the Kingdom* (New York: Harper and Row, 1981); Geervarghese Mar Osthathios, *Theology of a Classless Society* (Maryknoll, N. Y.: Orbis, 1980); and a fine dissertation study on the social nature of the Trinity by Cornelius Plantinga, Jr., which is soon to see print: "The Hodgson-Welch Debate and the Social Analogy of the Trinity" (Princeton Theological Seminary, 1982).

None, however, has approached the subject quite in the style of the present study. I have used an exegetical approach that owes a considerable debt to the critical analysis of persons, particularly in regard to the disclosure of their intention in speech and action. What I have tried to do is to look and see and to listen and try to understand what Jesus is doing and saying in the Gospel of John, and what he is intending to convey to his audience in regard to his relationship with the Father and the Holy Spirit, and with the new community comprised of his followers. This exegetical approach aims to be primarily descriptive of the speech, actions, and intention of Jesus in the fourth Gospel, with a view to understanding what he is saying about the divine Community and the new community of believers. Clearly the portrait of Jesus that the evangelist presents says something indirectly about his own belief in the person of Jesus Christ and what he wishes to convey to his readers about that faith. Hence a description of Jesus' speech, action, and intention in the Gospel of John will imply the evangelist's own estimate of Jesus' importance, both for himself and for his community of belief.

It is not required of the reader, therefore, that he or she necessarily agree with my high estimate of the evangelist's integrity in accurately reporting Jesus' words and acts to appreciate what Jesus is saying and doing in the storyline of the Gospel of John. As historians and interpreters of the fourth Gospel we may go in different directions, however, when we ask the next question, namely, whether this portrait of Jesus conforms to reality and genuinely describes what the historical Jesus really thought and said about himself and the divine Community, of which he claims in the Gospel to be the Son. If the biblical historian is confident that the Johannine portrait of Jesus does reflect Jesus' own intention and not just the intention of the evangelist, then a descriptive exegesis of Jesus' speech and action will tell us what he actually intended to say about the social nature of

God and reality. We come at this point to a third level of interpretation: whether the historian will accept Jesus' description of the way things are. If as interpreters we do not answer the question affirmatively, then neither the evangelist (level 1) nor Jesus (level 2) has much to say about the nature of reality at the third level. Biblical exegesis then becomes mainly an exercise in historical curiosity with little bearing on reality except as it performs a kind of psychohistorical analysis of what certain persons of the past subjectively thought about their world.

But of course it is not possible to interpret historical documents like the fourth Gospel without already assuming that the world is like this or like that, for hermeneutical assumptions are unavoidable and indispensable in reconstructing historical settings. The historian has to imagine what a particular context was like and what was possible before proceeding to describe the event. If the interpreter is suspicious of supernatural intervention and miracles, then these will be credited to the imagination of the author under study, not to historical fact. Hence the interpretation of history necessarily involves the world view of the historian, and becomes perforce a circular enterprise. One comes out where one goes in. There is not much that is neutrally scientific about it. As we were not present at events beyond our span of memory, we have to recreate past events imaginatively; and our minds are consciously or unconsciously committed to certain views of reality.

My point in reviewing this fact about historical research is simply to make my readers aware that I will assume their agreement with my descriptive analysis on level 1 (that the evangelist's faith is apparent in his portrait of Jesus' ministry in the Gospel). I will not assume that I will successfully carry everyone with me to the next level (that what Jesus says and does in the Gospel of John is historical); but I would underline that it is the intention of the evangelist to present himself as a reliable witness to historical fact (John 1:14; 15:27; 19:35; 21:24), and to invite the reader to accept his witness that Jesus actually said and did the things recorded of him in the Gospel and that he intended to be that kind of person. Entry to the third level is then not so difficult, if one has confidence that Jesus was speaking the truth. If the historian-exegete accepts Jesus' self-authenticating testimony about himself, then what Jesus says about the social nature of God and the world will have universal validity.

As a historian and exegete with Christian convictions, I find that noteworthy and distinguishing characteristics of the Triune Community emerge in Jesus' dialogues, and that an exegesis of the dialogues brings a new understanding of the social nature of God and the way in which New Testament life and ethics are grounded in the nature of the divine Triunity. Reflecting the divine Household, the household of the church is to demonstrate God's social nature and hospitality and being there at the disposal of others. Perhaps most impressive is the discovery that Jesus describes how Father, Son, and Spirit defer to one another and are at each other's disposal, and how they are redemptively at the disposal of the new community of believers. Accordingly, the ultimate grounding of Christian life and behavior is seen to lie in the social life and behavior of the persons of the divine Family who are there for one another in essential Triunity.

Before we turn to an exegesis of the divine Community in the Gospel of John there are important biblical themes to be highlighted that are helpful in understanding the nature of God's social reality as it appears in the fourth Gospel.

Biblical Backgrounds: Creation Converses Because God Converses

The Old and New Testaments consistently accentuate the importance of language (viz., intention, speech, action) and the purity of language in describing the essential nature of God and of creation. The point is demonstrated when one reads through the Bible from Genesis to Revelation and notes the number of passages that warn of the dire consequences of misusing language or exhort to proper use of language and its benefits. Throughout Scripture it is clear that the texture of language is woven into the very fabric of reality. God speaks not only to bring the world into being and to redeem it after it has fallen, but also speaks within himself as divine Community because he is the social God.

God is the God who speaks, as Father, Son, and Holy Spirit. Speaking and conversing in dynamic and inexhaustible fellowship is the essential hallmark of God's own reality.

Scripture also discloses that the human family, as well as the whole family of creation, reflects the divine Community of God in conversation. To be is to converse together creatively and faithfully in unity of thought and with richness of variety on many levels of intensity. The heart of reality, beginning with God who speaks, is the creative power to converse. Supremely God, then we who are made in the image of God, are defined in terms of speaking and conversing creatively. As we shall see, this is a major theme in the fourth Gospel as well as being thematic throughout Scripture. God's own triune reality is covenanted and social, and human reality is intended by God to follow this pattern of covenanted language. So is all of nature in the Isaianic and Pauline visions of the peaceable kingdom (Isa. 11:1–9; Rom. 8:18–39).

Scripture portrays God as speaker and converser who stands behind his words with absolute faithfulness and integrity, a fact attested by the faithful dialogue of Father and Son and the faithful presence of the Holy Spirit within the circle of divine conversation in the fourth Gospel. The social and conversational nature of God explains why the Triune Society invests man and woman with the power of conversing and creates them to complement one another and to bring forth their kind in human family. Scripture describes the tragic abuse of language through the fall when its divine source is challenged and unfaithfulness is substituted for faithfulness. The creature then desires to be hidden and private rather than social and responsive. In the fall the willfully seductive and destructive misuse of the gift of language leads to a loss of the power to converse creatively. It leads also to the abuse of sexuality, enmity between man and woman, parents and children, and destructive competition between families and families of nations and the families of nature.

The eschatological hope of Scripture declares the urgency of appropriating what God has done in Jesus Christ through the power of the Holy Spirit to redeem the fallen families of humankind and to draw them back into fellowship with the divine Community. In light of the restorative visions of Isaiah 11:1–9 and Romans 8:18–39 it is clear that God intends to undo Babel (Gen. 11:1–9) by way of Pentecost (Acts 2) and encompass all the redeemed families of creation in one extensive continuum of fellowship, whose ultimate purpose is to glorify God and enjoy him forever. Creation will then be freed from its bondage to futility and decay, when the language of creative conversation, openness, and participation will be restored to its rightful place at the center of all that is.

The Conversing God

Immediately in the first book of the Old Testament God is heard to be speaking. In Genesis 1:3 he speaks the first words of creation, calling into existence the radiance of created light: " 'Let there be light'; and there was light." God speaks again and calls forth the firmament and land and ornaments each of the three principal creations of light, firmament, and land with sun, moon and stars, fish and fowl, creatures of the earth, and man and woman. God who reveals himself at the genesis of the world is seen to be the intelligent creative Agent who multiplies social networks by speaking and investing his creation with the gift of speech appropriate to its various social levels ("the heavens are telling the glory of God" and "day to day pours forth speech," Ps. 19:1, 2). In the highest reality of the conversing and creative divine Community lies the principal clue to the social nature of God and of his creation.

God's own act of speaking in bringing forth the universe is a social act of the Triune Society. The Son of God is present at the framing of creation, as Paul declares in Colossians 1:15–20: Christ is the wisdom of God, in whom, through whom, and unto whom are all things. He is before all things, in him all things hold together; he is the eternally begotten before all creation, he is the beginning, the sum total, the head, the first fruits, "that in everything he might be preeminent." In this passage Paul is drawing out hidden nuances in the opening words of Genesis, "In the beginning"

($b^e reshith$), and interprets this beginning as divine Wisdom, Christ himself: In Christ God created the heavens and the earth. Paul sees him as the personified Wisdom of Proverbs 8:22, the mystery of God "in whom are hid all the treasures of wisdom and knowledge" (Col. 2:2–3).

The fourth Gospel also declares Christ to be the original Speaker, the Expression, the Logos who is one with God and was in the beginning with God. Christ the Word of God was present at the framing of the worlds: "All things were made through him, and without him was not anything made that was made. In him was life, and the life was the light of men" (John 1:3–4). And, as the author of Hebrews says, it is Christ, God's Son, who "reflects the glory of God and bears the very stamp of his nature, upholding the universe by his word of power" (Heb. 1:3; cf. 11:3).

It is accordingly the speaking God, the Father and the Son with the Spirit hovering over the waters (Gen. 1:2), who calls the universe into existence and creates and sustains the socially interwoven families of the earth. God is the original Community, the supreme Society. As the triune God he defines the nature of reality as social by leaving the signature of his social nature on everything that is. If it were not for the fact that human minds are bent and fallen they would be able to intuit and understand God's social nature and purpose in the shaping of creation: "Ever since the creation of the world his invisible nature, namely, his eternal power and deity, has been clearly perceived in the things that have been made. So that they are without excuse" (Rom. 1:20; cf. Ps. 19:1–4). In the search to discover the origin and the meaning and role of the human family (together with all the other ecologically interrelated families of earth), Scripture points to the divine Community that has left its imprint upon the universe. God as Father, Son, and Holy Spirit, the One in Many and the Many in One, is disclosed in Scripture as the Family of God. God is the Original, creation is the copy; God is the fundamental Theme, creation reverberates with variations on the theme.

We turn now for a closer look at the defining function of the gift of language in the human family as a reflection of its

11

defining power in the social life of God. Language is social and sociality is rendered possible by the gift of speech.

Language in Paradise: The First Human Family

The Genesis story discloses that the human family did not appear as the result of chance collocations of atoms but by design of the divine Family: "Let us make man in our image, after our likeness; and let them have dominion. . . . So God created man in his own image, in the image of God he created him; male and female he created them" (Gen. 1:26–27). In this important thematic text the generic terms *God* and *man* are defined in terms of social plurals (God is in the plural form, and the plural personal pronouns *us* and *our* identify the social nature and conversation of God; while "man" is actually "them," male and female in social communion (cf. the social term *man* in Gen. 5:2, which includes male and female). God creates man and woman in the image of the conversing divine Community (I take the plurals of Gen. 1:26–27 to be triune plurals, though others would interpret them as God-and-his-council plurals; in any event they indicate the social image in which male and female are created). They are invested with the power to speak, to converse and to communicate both vertically with God and laterally with each other, as well as with their children and with the creatures who are under the power of man to name. A speaking intimacy obtains from the very first appearance of man and woman, as God shares with them what is characteristic of his own nature, namely, the power to converse and to be social.

That is one of the images of God that is reflected in the first human family. Man and woman are invited by grace to share in conversation and fellowship and love with the divine Family. As subcreators in the image of God they are gifted to speak and to sing variations on the fundamental theme of inexhaustible love, with the power to invite new beings (their children) to life and to draw them into the circle of the social family where language, conversation, and song abound. In being fruitful and multiplying (Gen. 1:28), husband and wife imitate God's generosity in creating wider circles of family that are sustained and hallowed by fellowship with the Triune Family.

Thus in exegeting the role and status of the paradisal family in Genesis one discovers that the Author of creation is essentially the speaking and conversing God who generously brings new creatures into conversation from the fullness of his own conversation as Father, Son, and Holy Spirit. God is social and therefore essentially linguistic (in the ultimate sense that does not limit the communication of the Triune Society to discursive temporal language); for what makes sociality possible is the power of God to speak and to converse creatively as Triune Society.

The Loss of Paradisal Speech: The Atomizing of the Created Family in the Fall

The compressed account of the paradisal family in Genesis thrusts quickly forward to the tragedy of the fall. In order for the human family to function properly it must from its inception derive its power from above and not from below, from the creating and sustaining Family and not from any of the created families of nature. There is a proper order of priorities in Genesis 1 and 2 that places God in the highest role, man and woman in the next highest, with the animal kingdom and the whole realm of atomicity under their dominion (Gen. 1:18–30). Thus:

The Triune Family
The Human Family: Husband, Wife, Children
The Animal, Vegetable, and Atomic Families

The line of authority is downward, from top to bottom. The line of respect and obedience is upward, from bottom to top. In this originally "natural" system the hierarchy of families is covenanted by proper spoken and acted language on every level, as divinely established perimeters are honored. God's single warning that humans are not to eat of the tree of the knowledge of good and evil is spoken by a benevolent Creator for the good of his creatures, for God knows that

13

man and woman can know evil only by doing evil and that evil will bring the separation of death (Gen. 2:16–17).

The wisdom of God's warning is borne out in the fall described in Genesis 3. The serpentine distorter of language who has fallen out of fellowship with the Family of God infects paradise with the antisocial rebellion of doubt and pride and effectively atomizes the first human family, reversing the created order of authority. The adversary does not directly speak from above (though his intention is to usurp the place of God) but assumes the form of a subtle serpent among the wild animals and speaks deceptively from the ground below, contesting the wisdom and authority of God above: "Has God said?" The serpent attacks the human family by way of the lower appetites, engendering lust for food and for independent wisdom, thereby parasitically misusing the gift of language to question the Giver of language. Finding response in the woman and the man he henceforth renders impossible the purity of covenanted language in the human family, until God should speak again a word of grace and re-creation in the person of his Son.

The evil effect of broken language and unfaithful relationships is compellingly described in the story. Husband and wife now know evil because they have done evil. They have become evil by stepping outside the social bond of trust with the Family of God, claiming the right, at the serpent's instigation, to revise God's language in favor of the creature's. They have committed the sin of the great reversal by investing the created order with the right to define right and wrong, thereby assaulting the prerogative of sovereignty that belongs only to the divine Community.

The tragic consequences of breaking the social bond of trust fall upon the first human family. Husband and wife lose the innocent enjoyment of their bodies and cover their original beauty with aprons of fig leaves, introducing new patterns of prurience and lust. Husband and wife hide from God, seeking to be secret rather than social. Fear replaces trust. Accusation replaces responsibility, as man blames woman and woman blames serpent. The tragic rebellion of the first human family against the divine Family issues in the judgment that husband and wife are now condemned to

14

pain and toil and worst of all, condemned to death (Gen. 3:16–24). Because God's created order images his own social nature, the antisocial choice of the stewards of creation affects all of nature for bad from top to bottom. Creation has been turned upside down and the divine order reversed. The whole earth has now become subject to futility by God's judgment (Rom. 8:20), and paradise has been lost (Gen. 3:23–24). Now every creature of earth from the lowly atom to man and woman will follow a vector that resembles an inverted V, rising, peaking, then falling and perishing.

Christ's Redemption of the Human Family and of Right Speaking

The biblical drama of salvation begins with the divine Society's pronouncement of judgment upon all that is antisocial, and it continues to the last page of the Book of Revelation. Paul writes that the fall is not God's final word on the human family, nor is his subjection of the world to futility, for he has subjected it in hope (Rom. 8:20). Through the long Old Testament period of revelation with its vivid symbolism God was preparing for the fullness of time when he would send his Son to redeem the fallen human family "so that we might receive adoption as sons" (Gal. 4:5). For, says Paul, "the creation waits with eager longing for the revealing of the sons of God; for the creation was subjected to futility, not of its own will but by the will of him who subjected it in hope; because the creation itself will be set free from its bondage to decay and obtain the glorious liberty of the children of God" (Rom. 8:19–21).

The incarnation of the Son of God and his redeeming death on the cross and resurrection open the way to reclaiming the human family and regaining paradise. This is the fulfillment of God's original prophecy when he renders judgment on the first family and the serpent in Eden and says to the serpent, "I will put enmity between you and the woman, and between your seed and her seed; he shall bruise your head, and you shall bruise his heel" (Gen. 3:15).

Jesus' invasion of Satan the strong man's house and the release of his captives (Matt. 12:28–29 para.) signals the in-

15

auguration of the redemptive reign of God and the new age. Prophecy begins to find its fulfillment as the gospel of salvation is preached and the social God creates a new society of believers who are covenanted in faithful language and purity of heart and are adopted into the family of God. A number of consequences follow upon the inauguration of the new age that has come as a result of Christ's saving work. They demand a new way of looking at the world:

1. First, the Christian is described as living in tension between the old age that is passing away and the new age of the Spirit that is breaking in. The contest is between the pull of the inauthentic "I" which is the egocentric and rebellious self (the *sarx*) and the authentic "I" of the spiritual life in Christ (the *pneuma*, Rom. 7:14–25). There is an internal tension that places not only the individual Christian but also the individual Christian family under stress. Externally there are pressures from the conflict with the world, such that the Christian as an individual and as a member of a family can speak of being afflicted, but not crushed, "always carrying in the body the death of Jesus, so that the life of Jesus may also be manifested in our bodies" (2 Cor. 4:8–10). In light of the present conflict the Christian understands that neither his own life nor his circles of family life will be free of stress as long as the strong man's house is being invaded. Hence, the wisdom of traditional Christian nuptial vows, "for better, for worse; for richer, for poorer; in sickness and in health, till death do us part." In regard to the Christian family, the realism of the New Testament does not depict marriage as a constant source of sensual excitement and pleasure but, because of deep commitments in faithful service to the divine Family, a source of pain as well as pleasure (1 Cor. 7).

2. Yet there is also joyous optimism in the New Testament. In the struggle between selfish rebellion and loving commitment the inaugural reign of Christ will at last prove victorious, hence the Christian and the Christian family are to model in their social fidelity the age to come that is now breaking in. Insofar as they find the grace and power to do so, the Christian husband and wife and their children are to evince the love and creative fidelity that is characteristic of

the body of Christ (Eph. 5:22–6:4). The Christian leader is to know how to manage his own household if he is to care for God's church (1 Tim. 3:1–7). Since Christians are fundamentally optimists because of what Christ has done and will do, "we do not lose heart." Indeed, says Paul,

> though our outer nature is wasting away, our inner nature is being renewed every day. For this slight momentary affliction is preparing for us an eternal weight of glory beyond all comparison, because we look not to the things that are seen but to the things that are unseen; for the things that are seen are transient, but the things that are unseen are eternal. [2 Cor. 4:16–18]

3. On the basis of this realism combined with optimism, Christians are exhorted to take their temporal and human families seriously and their covenant responsibilities earnestly. This means that they are to consider wives and husbands and children, parents and extended families—and indeed all of humankind—in a social and Christ-like way. Christians are to regard no one from a limited and selfish human point of view (2 Cor. 5:16) but are to see with the eyes of Christ the inclusive family that exists on a higher level. On this level of a new social awareness, a person who is in Christ "is a new creation, the old has passed away, behold, the new has come" (2 Cor. 5:17).

Accordingly, the new family life in Christ is superimposed on the fading earthly family, where age and entropy take their toll and distance and death finally separate in what would otherwise be tragic loss. The temporary earthly family, residually beautiful because of God's original creation but subject to wasting because of the fall, is given new meaning when its members are seen to be children of God as they manifest faith in Christ. As spiritual members of the larger family of God, Christians are seen to be parts of the whole, whose head is Christ (1 Cor. 12:12; Eph. 4:15–16). He is the Vine, believers are the branches (John 15:5). The social metaphors are prominent. In Christ, writes Peter, "you are a chosen race, a royal priesthood, a holy nation, God's own people, that you may declare the wonderful deeds of him

17

who called you out of darkness into his marvelous light" (1 Peter 2:9).

Because the social pattern of the divine Community is superimposed upon the new community of believers, there are other biblical teachings that follow:

4. Since believers in Christ become children in the family of God (Rom. 8:16–17), marriage and children are not the only gifts of God's social grace in the higher family. Singleness is also a gift to those so called, as Paul makes clear in 1 Corinthians 7:7, 17, 38, 40 (cf. Jesus' teaching, Matt. 19:10–12). Man and woman are called as Christians to marriage or to singleness by the sovereign grace of God within the social network of the family, where each makes a contribution: "Each has his own special gift from God, one of one kind and one of another" (1 Cor. 7:7). "Let every one lead the life which the Lord has assigned to him, and in which God has called him" (v. 17; cf. 1 Cor. 12:4–31). Paul's point is that every individual Christian belongs essentially to the family of God, not to himself or herself, and must seek the Lord's leading concerning the pattern of life to be led within the divine family. To be a Christian is to be a social person because God is essentially social. One's calling may be to marriage and children, which is the usual pattern and was for most of the original apostles (1 Cor. 9:5); or it may be to the single life as a servant in God's higher family in service of his created family, as was the case with Paul (1 Cor. 7:7–8) and our Lord himself (Matt. 19:11). In either case the speech and actions of the Christian are to be socially covenanted in Christ, with sexuality either sublimated for his will or expressed within the covenant responsibilities of marriage and the human family. Christians have been bought with a price (1 Cor. 7:23; 6:19) and accordingly are to glorify God in their bodies within the body.

5. There is however an eschatological sense of urgency within the social life of the body of Christ in view of the fact that the new age has been inaugurated by Jesus and moves forward to an imminent completion. Hence if Christians are married they are not to consider husband, wife, or children to be substitutes in any sense for the divine Family, which would be idolatry, but are to place the human family in

proper perspective. Husband, wife, or children must not be ends in themselves; indeed, a higher loyalty to the Triune Family compels the members of the Christian earthly family to appreciate its temporality and the fact that husband, wife, and children have eternal value in this present age only because they are part of the larger family from which all lesser families are derived. Paul makes a radical but altogether logical appeal that husband and wife—all Christians in fact—should live with a radical eschatological vision: "From now on, let those who have wives live as though they had none, and those who mourn as though they were not mourning, and those who rejoice as though they were not rejoicing, and those who buy as though they had no goods, and those who deal with the world as though they had no dealings with it. For the form of this world is passing away" (1 Cor. 7:29–31).

Christians are not to live as though the institutions and patterns of this world were ultimate, for that would be living *kata sarka*, according to a human or fallen point of view (2 Cor. 5:16). Paradoxically, as Jesus taught, a person finds genuine and lasting life only in losing this life, that is, in not making it ultimate, and loses life in pursuing it as ultimate (Matt. 16:24–26). A false and ultimately self-destructive pursuit therefore is any sort of preoccupation with self-actualization that avoids the social nature of reality and ultimate responsibility to the Triune Family. When Christians seek first the higher Family they discover the real worth and position of the human family and all the other families of the created order which take on a covenanted value that transposes them from above. "But seek first his kingdom and his righteousness," says Jesus, "and all these things shall be yours as well" (Matt. 6:33). The lasting worth of earthly families can be appreciated only by acknowledging God's disclosure that the original Family has invested them with social value.

6. Accordingly, the Christian husband and wife and their children, together with the single Christian, belong to a higher family and are to serve the First Family with creative fidelity. This social fidelity is to be lived out in the following pattern:

a. First, the Christian body of believers who have been called into being by the hospitality of the social God are to be faithful in proclaiming the good news that God is calling home the disparate families of earth who have been estranged from the divine Community and from each other since the rebellion of Eden and Babel. At Pentecost (Acts 2) the Holy Spirit begins to restore the bent languages of humankind to unity and straightness by the proclamation of what God has accomplished though Jesus the Son on the cross and in the resurrection. Faithful speech is restored in regenerate hearts, estranged persons are brought back together, husbands and wives and their children find new dimensions of love and faithfulness, and single persons no longer live under the stigma of loneliness or barrenness. All discover a new fecundity and unity in speaking and preaching the saving Word by which God sovereignly draws the lost and the lonely to himself and adopts them as sons and daughters into his First Family. In preaching the socially reconciling Word, the children of God seek to purify human institutions and protect the delicate social networks of the created order, anticipating their restoration to paradisal patterns of harmony at the end of the age.

b. Second, each believing member who is ingrafted into the First Family is exhorted to live according to God's eschatological design for life, exhibiting in every dimension of redeemed language (intention, speech, and action) the healing effect of the new social covenant in Christ. Christians are to be ambassadors for Christ, God making his appeal through them as they work out the ministry of reconciliation (2 Cor. 5:18–21). Every Christian as a member of God's family is to manifest the fruit of the Spirit—"love, joy, peace, patience, kindness, goodness, faithfulness, gentleness, self-control" (Gal. 5:22–23). Because the Christian belongs to a higher realm where God the Architect and Archetype of Family is sovereign, married and single Christians cannot consider alternative styles of life practiced by a world that is turned in upon itself and bent on individual self-gratification (Gal. 5:16–21). The goal of Christian families and the higher family of Christ's body is not to get but to give, not to destroy the social gift that reflects the social nature of God but to articulate it as it comes to expression through the ministering of the Holy Spirit. By word and example Christians are to invite others into the circle of love and healing where faithful speech becomes the vehicle of grace for communion with the conversing God and with a universe that declares the glory of God.

An essential characteristic of the divine Community is revealed through the mind of Christ, which Paul describes in Philippians 2:1–11. It is the quality of being there for the other, of being at one another's disposal. As this defines the mind of Christ so, writes Paul, it should define the attitude of Christians. It is the essential key to understanding the social nature of the Triune Family. As will become clear in our exegesis of the Gospel of John, each of the persons of the Trinity is at the service of the others, so united are they in essential love. Each of the persons of the Trinity is also at the disposal of the new community of believers, as Christ the speaker for the divine Community proclaims in speech and act. If God is like that, Christians should aspire to nothing less than to be complete or perfect (*teleioi*) as God is complete and perfect in social love (Matt. 5:48). In redeeming the world and showing what it means for God to be at our disposal, Christ the Son eminently embodies the quality of divine disposability. He demonstrates that the way up is the way down through servanthood. This becomes the essential pattern that defines Christian social behavior. In Gospels and Epistles, in Acts and Revelation, Christian ethics are grounded in the social disposability of the incarnate Christ, who embodies the hospitality of the divine Society.

7. The redemptive work of the Triune Family extends to the families of creation that were called into being before the appearance of man and woman. In chiastic fashion (*a b b' a'*), where *a* is creation, *b* is Adam and *b'* is Christ the new Adam, *a'* becomes the final redemption of original creation that is to take place at the close of the age. The fall of Adam and Eve carried nature with them, and as a consequence of the inexorable justice and mercy of God "the creation was subjected to futility, not of its own will but by the will of him who subjected it in hope" (Rom. 8:20). God's righteous judgment of sinful Adam extended to all creation because

creation was originally designed by the Triune Family to be an interwoven family of families, man and woman serving as God's vicegerents and caretakers. When the first human beings defaulted in their role, the divine Community subjected creation to futility, but also in hope. In the fullness of time (Mark 1:15; Gal. 4:4; Eph. 1:10; Luke 4:21) the Father sent the Son in the power of the Holy Spirit to inaugurate the season of hope. In the great social act of divine disposability at the hinge of history, which was Jesus' death and resurrection, the Triune God laid the futility of condemned creation upon himself, propitiated his own righteous wrath against evil by the most precious and costly gift of the Son (Rom. 3:21–26), and turned the direction of creation around, away from futility to hope.

The first Adam carried creation down with him. The second Adam carries creation up with him: "the creation itself will be set free from its bondage to decay and obtain the glorious liberty of the children of God" (Rom. 8:21). This new time which the Triune Family has inaugurated affords opportunity for Christians to groan redemptively with the groaning of creation as it travails from futility to hope. Creation groans and "we ourselves, who have the first fruits of the Spirit, groan inwardly as we wait for adoption as sons, the redemption of our bodies" (Rom. 8:23). What is remarkable about this groaning (the Greek root of which is the stem *sten*) is that "the Spirit himself intercedes for us with groans that words cannot express" (Rom. 8:26, NIV). The divine Community groans with gracious disposability to bring a fallen creation to social perfection.

The biblical disclosure declares that the time of social redemption is in process of realization through the saving grace of Father, Son, and Holy Spirit, the divine Community. The new age has been inaugurated and Christians enjoined to minister the redemptive work to all the families of earth, in anticipation of the day when the visions of Isaiah and Paul are realized and when, in the vision of John the Seer (Rev. 21:1; 22:2–3), the tree of life, untouched and untouchable since the fall, will yield its fruit for eating and its leaves for the healing of the nations.

2

The Divine Community in the Fourth Gospel
John 1–7

We have made some preliminary observations on the social relationship of Father, Son, and Holy Spirit in Scripture. Now we turn our attention to specific passages in the Gospel of John to see how mutual loving, generosity, glorification, equality, availability, disposability, and deference characterize the divine Family in the Gospel as a whole. The key to the deference that Jesus continually shows to the Father is to be found in two facts that emerge from an exegesis of the texts. First, we will notice that whenever Jesus defers to the Father as the one who has sent him and given him his message, he almost always balances this deference with a claim of equality with the Father. Second, the reason for his deference is stated clearly by Jesus to offset any charge that he is speaking boastfully as a false prophet from a human point of view:

7:18   "He who speaks on his authority
           seeks his own glory;
       but he who seeks the glory of him who sent him
           is true,
       and in him there is no falsehood."

There is no falsehood in Jesus because his whole life is devoted to the glorification of the Father. He is totally available to him. Hence the authority by which Jesus uses the personal pronoun *I* and claims equality with the Father is tempered by a deferential attitude that reflects an essential characteristic of the divine Community as a whole. Each person of the Triunity not only shares equality with the other persons of the divine Community but also defers in their honor and stands at their disposal for their glorification. As we shall see later on in our study, this fundamental attitude of being there for the sake of the other is intended to be a defining characteristic of believers as they image the divine Family in their personal relationships.

The Incarnate Word
Chapter 1

The prologue of the Gospel sounds an elevated theme and asserts that Jesus the incarnate Son is to be identified with the eternal Logos who is with God and is God, through whom life and light flow into the world of darkness. The opening theme concerns the equality of the heavenly Family. The second clause of verse 1 describes the social relationship of the Word and God, while the third clause identifies their unity and is not to be translated "and the Word was divine," but correctly "and the Word was God," for the context and Greek style require it (in the New Testament the article is often omitted when the definite noun precedes the verb, as here):

1:1 In the beginning was the Word,
and the Word was with God,
and the Word was God (*kai theos ēn ho logos*).
1:2 He was in the beginning with God:
1:3 all things were made through him,
and without him was not anything made
that was made.
1:4 In him was life,
and the life was the light of men.
1:5 The light shines in the darkness,
and the darkness has not overcome it.

The transposition of the Word into his own creation is thematically expressed in 1:14 as a genuine historical incarnation. In Jesus, the Son of the Father, we behold the Word embodied in time and space, full of grace and truth:

1:14   And the Word became flesh
        and dwelt among us,
        full of grace and truth;
    we have beheld his glory,
        glory as of the only Son from the Father.

The theme of the incarnate Word is stated with great clarity. Jesus is the representative of the Family of God in human flesh. John the Baptist bears witness to Jesus' preexistence in ironic verse, for although Jesus temporally comes after John he actually outranks him as the preexistent Son:

1:15   "He who comes after me
        ranks before me,
        for he was before me."

The evangelist acclaims the fullness of the incarnate Son from which believers have all received "grace upon grace" (1:16). In Jesus the embodied Son the invisible God becomes personally known in time and space. Verse 18 equates the Son with God the Father and should be translated according to the stronger textual evidence:

1:18   No one has ever seen God;
        [the only begotten God] (*monogenēs theos;* RSV,
            the only Son),
      who is in the bosom of the Father,
        he has made him known.

This verse evidences the unity of Father and Son and their warm deference to one another in making the divine Family known to the world. The text implies that the Father honors the Son by sending him to do what has never been done before in history, namely, for God to reveal himself visibly in human form. It also implies that the Son honors the Father in taking on human flesh in order to make him known. The image of the only begotten God resting in the bosom (*kolpos*) of the Father should be construed as a family image. The human concept of a son resting in the bosom of his father is heightened to infinite proportions to define the relationship

25

of Father and Son in the divine Community. This heightening is possible from the human side because creation has been invested with valid analogies from the divine side. It is because God the Creator is social that creation is social and can be used of God to direct the creature upward to the real source of community and family, for the Triune God is the principal Community and Family. Thus upon reflection, verse 18 is a powerful revelation of the intimate family relationship of Father and Son, and of their equality, mutual respect, and interpersonal communion.

The Testimony of John the Baptist to Jesus

Any suggestion that Jesus' submission to the Father's will and his association with John the Baptist might shed some light on Jesus' religious development in earlier stages of his life and ministry is put to rest by the Baptist's disclaimer that Jesus is greater than he. As a charismatically inspired prophet John defines his role and that of Jesus in terms that clearly delineate the inferiority of the one and the superiority of the other. In prophetic utterance John may have spoken more than he fully understood, but there is no reason not to take his pronouncements as historically accurate if we accept scriptural testimony that the Holy Spirit ministers with inspired utterances at his discretion in moments of special revelation. Accordingly, the Baptist's disclaimer that he is not the Christ (1:20) but "the voice of one crying in the wilderness" to make straight the way of the Lord (1:23), serving as the Messiah's forerunner and baptizing with water, is signed and sealed with two contrasting statements, one referring to himself, the other to Jesus. In the first, John lowers himself below the ordinary servant who washes the feet of the honored guest. He says,

1:26   "Among you stands one whom you do not know,
1:27   even he who comes after me,
        the thong of whose sandal I am not worthy to
          untie."

In the second, the Baptist observes Jesus coming toward him and says,

26

1:29   "Behold, the Lamb of God,
             who takes away the sin of the world!"

In both instances John the Baptist is inspired to employ
images that define two levels of servanthood. He is the servant who is unworthy, on his own admission, of unloosing
Jesus' sandal, while Jesus is the servant Lamb who is worthy
of unloosing the sin of the world. These are not utterances
placed on John's lips at a later time by the evangelist; otherwise the Gospel's theme of the incarnate Word (established
in 1:14) would be countermanded and a docetic or gnostic
approach substituted for the incarnational. The evangelist
implies that we are dealing here with real history and the
drama of God establishing roles and levels of status at the
beginning of Jesus' ministry as the Son embodies the saving
grace of the divine Community.

The Divine Family at the Inaugural Baptism
of the Son

The function of the Triune Family at the beginning of
Jesus' ministry is dramatically described by John the Baptist, who is eyewitness at the inaugural baptism of Jesus. It
is important to take the words of 1:32, "And John bore witness," seriously as an eyewitness account of something that
occurs between Father, Son, and Holy Spirit at the inauguration of Jesus' ministry, when the divine Community expresses unity and approval in the anointing of Jesus for the
work of redemption. Although the baptism in Jordan is not
expressly mentioned, every indication is that it is implied in
the contrast of John's baptism with water and the baptism
of Jesus with the Holy Spirit. In 1:32–34 the Baptist explicitly claims to have seen this event of Jesus' anointing, in
fulfillment of a word of prophecy personally given to him by
the Lord himself prior to the occasion:

1:32   And John bore witness,
             "I saw the Spirit descend as a dove from
                 heaven,
                 and it remained on him.

27

1:33   I myself did not know him;
             but he who sent me to baptize with water
               said to me,
             'He on whom you see the Spirit descend and
               remain,
               this is he who baptizes with the Holy
               Spirit.'
1:34   And I have seen and borne witness
             that this is the Son of God."

That John the Baptist has seen the dove descend upon Jesus means that the divine anointing is not only a subjective experience of Jesus but also demonstrable evidence in time and space that Jesus is truly the incarnate Son of God who receives the approval of the divine Family. At the same time, John's attestation that the dove remains on Jesus implies that he is given to see the inner dimension of this historical event: Jesus will continue throughout his ministry to manifest the baptism of the Holy Spirit (this in spite of the Baptist's later question as to what the baptism of the Holy Spirit entailed, cf. Matt. 11:2–6 para.). All four Gospels agree that at the beginning of Jesus' ministry the Triune Family is present to inaugurate the new time of salvation, Father and Spirit deferring to the Son who is to act as spokesman for the divine Community, and the Son deferring to the Father and the Spirit in accepting their commission to represent the one gracious will of the divine Family (cf. Matt. 3:11–17; Mark 1:9–11; Luke 3:21–22). All three persons of the Triune Family are in complete harmony in placing themselves, through the representative person of the Son, at the disposal of sinners who need salvation. Accordingly, the baptism of Jesus appears in this Gospel, as in the others, as one of the great events in historical time and space when the divine Community acts as one to redeem a fallen creation and draw it back into fellowship with the higher Family.

Jesus, Son of God and Son of Man

Prophetic utterance is also given Nathanael to describe Jesus through charismatic insight:

1:49   "Rabbi, you are the Son of God!
You are the King of Israel!"

Again, these words are not later redactions of the pious community. The phenomenon of prophetic inspiration is functioning here, as with John the Baptist, and we miss the controlling motif of 1:14, "And the Word became flesh," if we do not allow the Holy Spirit to bear witness to the incarnate Son through inspired speech. Jesus responds to Nathanael's inspired utterance with his own prophetic declaration:

1:51   "Truly, truly, I say to you,
you will see heaven opened,
and the angels ascending and descending
upon the Son of man."

We need not imagine that John the Baptist or Nathanael, or any of the others who are mentioned in the gospel sources as uttering inspired speech, understood fully what they were saying. In time they would, but for now their prophetic insights ring changes on the fundamental theme of Jesus who does know who he is. He knows that he is the Son of God and the Son of man. This ringing of the changes on the basic motif of 1:14 allows the evangelist to select his materials from a rich treasury of eyewitness accounts and to fulfill his immediate purpose of writing a Gospel, "that you may believe that Jesus is the Christ, the Son of God, and that believing you may have life in his name" (20:31), directed to believers and nonbelievers alike.

Jesus as Son of Mary and Son of the Father
Chapter 2

That Jesus knows who he is and is not described by the evangelist as struggling to discover himself religiously helps us understand his impatience with his mother's query at the wedding at Cana ("O woman, what have you to do with me? My hour has not yet come" [2:4]). This seems a strange reply, but when compared with his similarly odd response at age twelve to his parents at the temple in Jerusalem ("How is it that you sought me? Did you not know that I must be in my Father's house?" [Luke 2:49]), the matter is clarified. In both instances Jesus evidences a conscious sense of higher sonship. Pride of place is to be given to the Father with whom he is in one accord. Even near the age of bar mitzvah Jesus has come to this sense of faithfulness to the Father and does nothing that is not in accord with the will of his higher Family. He places himself at their disposal first. Nonetheless, the fact that on each occasion he makes himself available for others reflects the reason for his coming and the generous redemptive disposition of the divine Family on behalf of those in need. Having made his point about his prior relationship to the Father, he obeys his parents (Luke 2:51), and having made his point about his coming hour, which Mary does not understand in her implied request for a small miracle at the marriage at Cana, Jesus complies and makes himself generously available to the wedding guests. But he transposes the incident to a higher level, using the transformation of water into wine as a sign, manifesting his glory and eliciting belief in his disciples (2:11). Jesus becomes the master of transposition as he uses ordinary things in common circumstances to draw the viewer to association with his higher Family.

We see this happening in the first of his temple cleansings at the beginning of his ministry. There are two cleansings in the gospel accounts, appropriately framing the beginning and the ending of his redemptive ministry on behalf of the divine Family to purify the house of dwelling. Jesus' oneness with the Father and his distinctive claim to represent him and his dwelling place is apparent in this cleansing of the temple. Jesus utters an unusual prophetic statement in which he claims equality with the Father yet evidences his faithful disposability to him by cleansing his earthly temple, prophesying its destruction and the raising up of the real temple, namely, himself:

2:16   "Take these things away;
         you shall not make my Father's house
         a house of trade."

2:19   "Destroy this temple,
        and in three days I will raise it up."

In his prophetic act of cleansing and speaking, something odd is going on that Jesus understands but his disciples do not, until later. Hence the explanatory words of the evangelist, who confirms that Jesus knew who he was and what he was doing, even if they did not:

2:22   When therefore he was raised from the dead,
        his disciples remembered that he had said this;
           and they believed the scripture
           and the word which Jesus had spoken.

John acknowledges that for the disciples the resurrection was the key that unlocked the meaning of Jesus' prophecy on the occasion of the temple cleansing. Only after its fulfillment did they understand what Jesus had meant. Jesus understood it beforehand. Yet they remembered that he had said this, and that attests its historicity and that Jesus had understood himself in such extraordinary terms. They came to understand that Jesus had been conscious of such a close filial relationship with the Father that he could speak of the temple as "my Father's house," in deference to the Father (2:16), while naming himself as the very temple itself in the truest sense ("Destroy this temple, and in three days I will raise it up" [2:19]). Jesus claimed personal possession of the temple as Son of the Father, cleansed it in a prophetically parabolic act of generosity, and made it once again available for prayer, prophesying that the transition from the earthly temple to the temple of his own person was already underway and would be completed at his coming resurrection from the dead.

In his act of cleansing Jesus fulfilled Old Testament prophecy (Zech. 14:21; Mal. 3:1–3; Ps. 69:9; Isa. 56:7) and identifies himself as representative of the Father, while remaining at the disposal of the Father as faithful Son. "Destroy this temple" bears a double meaning and refers ironically to both temples, but particularly to the temple who is Jesus. He is conscious from the beginning of his ministry that he is the actual dwelling place of the Father, available on behalf of believers who are to come and live there. Ironically but prophetically the misunderstanding of "destroy this temple" on the part of the authorities leads to Jesus' crucifixion, on the charge of blasphemy—that he has sought the destruction of the physical temple (Matt. 26:61; 27:40 para.). The irony is that only by the destruction of Jesus' temple at his crucifixion, as he makes himself wholly disposable to the world of sinners, can the temple of his person be raised again. The old temple of stone is destined for final destruction. Henceforth the Father dwells among his people only in the temple of his Son.

Jesus and Nicodemus: The Love of the Triune Family for the World
Chapter 3

John the evangelist describes the close connection between Father and Son in Jesus' discourse with Nicodemus and defines the love of God for the world as the Father's gift of his only begotten Son. Believing in him means that one will not perish but will be saved and have eternal life (3:16–17). Without belief in the only Son of God, one is condemned already (3:18, 36). Jesus the Son of God is equal to the Father in righteousness (cf. 5:18), while Father and Son are characterized by generosity and availability to each other and to the world. Jesus makes clear that the divine Community works as one to redeem the lost, for the Spirit is also at work in bringing about an experience of new birth: "Unless one is born of water and the Spirit, he cannot enter the kingdom of God" (3:5; cf. vv. 3–4, 6–8). Jesus identifies the kingdom of God with life in himself (3:15–16), and since he is the Son of man (3:13–14) and the Son of God (3:16–18), the complete circle of the divine Family is present in the work of redemption. Father, Son, and Spirit serve as one as they make themselves available for the lost.

The Baptist's discourse to his disciples, in response to their query concerning Jesus' ministry, provides further prophetic confirmation of Jesus' equality with the Father.

John sees Jesus as the bridegroom and himself as the friend of the bridegroom (3:29). This image implies that both John the Baptist and Jesus understand that Jesus the bridegroom is fulfilling the Old Testament hope of God's returning in the new age to take his bride once again to himself (Hos. 2:16–20). In light of this, John utters the ultimate personal disclaimer, "He must increase, but I must decrease" (3:30). He then prophesies with inspired address that links Father, Son, and Spirit in the redemptive disclosure of the divine Community:

3:34   "For he whom God has sent utters the words of God,
        for it is not by measure that he gives the Spirit."

This is followed by an equality saying that illustrates the loving deference of the Father to the Son in sharing all the divine prerogatives:

3:35   "the Father loves the Son,
        and has given all things into his hand."

One implication of the disclosure that Jesus has all things in his hand is that the future of every person is determined by personal response to the Son. Father and Spirit defer to the Son as the focus of the Triune Family in respect to the salvation or the judgment of every human being:

3:36   "He who believes in the Son has eternal life;
        he who does not obey the Son shall not see life,
            but the wrath of God rests upon him."

Accordingly, the line of generosity, availability, disposability, and submission within the divine Family does not run in one direction only, that is, only from Son to Father, but is reciprocal and symmetrical, as this text affirms. It will be important to keep this and other similar passages in mind as we continue to exegete the Gospel for the light it sheds on the nature of the Triune Family. A clear pattern is emerging that the Triune God is internally social, hence externally social in creation and redemption. Availability and disposability, that is, a willingness to be there in service of the other, appears to be the hallmark of Father, Son, and Holy Spirit, and a characteristic that identifies their essential oneness.

Jesus and the Samaritan Woman
Chapter 4

Jesus' discourse with the Samaritan woman at Jacob's well again affirms his consciousness of having a special filial relationship with the Father. In this episode he represents the Father fully and can refer to himself in terms of equality with the Father. Jesus' use of the personal pronoun *I* is indicative of his sense of authority, as he claims to be the living water that saves to eternal life:

4:14   "Whoever drinks of the water that I shall give
                 him
            will never thirst;
        the water that I shall give him
            will become in him a spring of water
                welling up to eternal life."

As the conversation with the woman intensifies and touches upon the differences between Jewish and Samaritan worship, Jesus speaks of what true worship of the Father entails and reveals himself as the Messiah, implying that it is through him that the Father will be truly worshiped. Replying to her remark that she knows the Messiah is coming and will show us all things, Jesus declares:

4:26   "I who speak to you am he."

The progression of Jesus' self-disclosure in the story is noteworthy. He first reveals himself as the one who satisfies spiritual thirst (4:7–15), then as the one who sees into the heart and speaks truthfully about the spiritual condition of the woman (4:16–18), then as the prophet who describes true worship of the Father as spiritual and not geographical

(4:20–22), and finally as the self-revealed Messiah who claims that the hour of the true worshiper, whether Jew or Samaritan, is now in terms of himself, thereby linking his own person with that of the Father (4:23–26). The hour of reconciliation with the Father is not only coming but is now present in the person of Jesus the Son. Jesus draws out the implications of this inaugurated eschatology in his response to his disciples' invitation to eat. Just as ordinary water serves as a means to illustrate the higher spiritual living water that is Jesus himself, ordinary food serves as an image of the original life-giving relationship of Father and Son:

4:32 "I have food to eat of which you do not know."

4:34 "My food is to do the will of him who sent me, and to accomplish his work."

Typically, Jesus places his personal claim to authority alongside his submission to the will of the Father. The two themes are like alternating current in the relationship of the persons of the divine Community and reflect their essential oneness. The effect upon the created order is substantial. Because the Father's will is realized in Jesus the Son, the coming age is now inaugurated, sinners are invited home, disciples are invited to lift up their eyes to fields already white for harvest (4:35–38), and the hitherto excluded Samaritans believe (4:39–42).

Jesus' Claims at Bethesda
Chapter 5

The presence of the Father's generosity in Jesus the Son and the offense of his claim to be equal to the Father are illustrated in the event that surrounds his healing of the lame man at the pool of Bethesda on the sabbath. Jesus is accused by the religious authorities of profaning the sabbath by working a healing. To this Jesus replies:

5:17 "My Father is working still, and I am working."

Not only is Jesus making the point that when it comes to healing the lost God observes no sabbaths, but also he is equating his work with the work of the Father. The authorities catch the connection and conspire all the more to get rid of him,

5:18   because he not only broke the sabbath
        but also called God his Father,
        making himself equal with God.

Immediately upon his claim of equality with God the Father in working the same work, Jesus expresses the complementary other half of the social relationship that characterizes Father and Son. There is such coordinate unity between them that the Son acts just like the Father and would never think of doing anything without being in one accord with him:

5:19   "Truly, truly, I say to you,
        the Son can do nothing of his own accord,
        but only what he sees the Father doing;
        for whatever he does,
        that the Son does likewise."

Similarly, love binds Father and Son together in mutual sharing, so that Jesus discloses the continuous working of the divine Community as his ministry unfolds:

5:20   "For the Father loves the Son,
        and shows him all that he himself is doing;
        and greater works than these will he show him,
        that you may marvel."

As the Father is generous to the world so the Son is generous to the world. Father and Son share in the exercise of life-giving power:

5:21   "For as the Father raises the dead and gives them life,
        so also the Son gives life to whom he will."

36

The Father also defers to the Son in giving him all authority to judge. The Father submits to the good judgment of the
Son and trusts his judgment completely. Jesus the Son
claims equal honor with the Father, presents himself as the
standard by which the Father is honored, claims to be sent
from the Father, yet defers to the Father by making it clear
that he is sent:

5:22   "The Father judges no one,
        but has given all judgment to the Son,
5:23   that all may honor the Son,
        even as they honor the Father.
    He who does not honor the Son
        does not honor the Father who sent him."

Again, Jesus equates his word with the word of the Father
and defines salvation in terms of one's honoring that word
by believing in the Father who has sent the Son. Father and
Son are mutually at one another's service in the work of
salvation, while the fact that the believer receives eternal
life as a result of belief is evidence that Father and Son are
at the service of the believer:

5:24   "Truly, truly, I say to you,
        he who hears my word
        and believes him who sent me,
          has eternal life;
        he does not come into judgment,
          but has passed from death to life."

Expressing the generosity of the divine Community, Jesus
claims that the promised hour of salvation is coming and
now is, is not yet and already, because it has been inaugurated in him. It is in terms of his voice, the voice of the Son
of God, that the dead will hear and will live. Jesus makes no
distinction between the voice of God and his own voice. As
the Son of God he speaks on behalf of the divine Community,
implying not only his divine equality but also his representative disposability on behalf of believers:

5:25   "Truly, truly, I say to you,
the hour is coming, and now is,
when the dead will hear the voice of the Son
of God,
and those who hear will live."

The mutual interdependence of Father and Son is further clarified as Jesus describes the generosity of the Father in sharing life equally with the Son, so that there is absolute parity between them. Once more Jesus makes it clear that he also shares equal authority with the Father to judge. He implies that because he has been willing to represent the divine Family as the Son of man, he is worthy of executing divine judgment, hence the Father willingly subordinates himself to the Son. Presently Jesus will say that this judgment is not his own but what he hears from the Father (5:30), but at this moment he is asserting his power and his right to judge:

5:26   "For as the Father has life in himelf,
so he has granted the Son also to have life in
himself,
5:27   and has given him authority to execute
judgment,
because he is the Son of man."

After pronouncing a word of prophecy regarding those who will come forth from the tombs when they hear his voice, as evildoers will be raised to judgment (5:28–29), Jesus expresses the other side of the formula by submitting completely to the Father. As we have noted, this is one of the most remarkable characteristics of the divine Community, to assert authority and at the same time to become completely subordinate to one another. It is the key to the divine nature and it is the key to the nature of the redeemed community. The ultimate paradox is to express individuality while listening responsively to the other, being one in thought and purpose. In his language Jesus modulates from one to the other with perfect ease because he exemplifies the relational nature of the divine Family:

5:30   "I can do nothing on my own authority;
        as I hear, I judge;
        and my judgment is just,
           because I seek not my own will
           but the will of him who sent me."

If Jesus were putting himself forward as an independent individual he would falsify the essentially relational and social nature of the divine Community. That is why, having made astounding claims to divine authority, he discounts any suspicion that he might be making a selfish claim to independence from the Father. Since he does in fact defer to the Father, his witness is identical to the Father's, for the Father bears witness to him:

5:31   "If I bear witness to myself,
        my testimony is not true;
5:32   there is another who bears witness to me,
        and I know that the testimony which he bears
           to me is true."

This sheds light on Jesus' saying in 8:14: "Even if I do bear witness to myself, my testimony is true, for I know whence I have come and whither I am going." Jesus does bear witness to himself, but he does it only in oneness with the will of the divine Family. In 5:31 he has in mind any witness that might be self-seeking and independent of Family unity. That he totally repudiates.

Jesus turns to the Baptist's witness and observes how this prophet of God has shown deference to the superiority of the Son. He has borne witness to Jesus as the light (1:6–8), he has acknowledged that Jesus is of higher rank (1:15), he has referred to him as Lord (1:23), Lamb of God (1:29, 36), and Son of God (1:34). John the Baptist does not claim that he knows this of himself, but that it is divinely revealed to him (1:32–34). Jesus also makes this point and defers to John's witness only for the sake of believers:

5:33   "You sent to John, and he has borne witness to
        the truth.

5:34   Not that the testimony which I receive is from
                    man;
             but I say this that you may be saved."

In fact, however, the Father's witness to the Son is greater than John's, for the Son's works attest that they are of the Father. Equality of Father and Son is indicated by the respect the Father shows the Son in sending him to do his works, and by the respect the Son shows the Father in accomplishing his works. Jesus contrasts his testimony with that of the Baptist and claims that his own is far greater because the Son represents the Father:

5:35   "He was a burning and shining lamp,
                    and you were willing to rejoice for a while in
                        his light.
5:36   But the testimony which I have
                    is greater than that of John;
             for the works which the Father has granted me to
                    accomplish,
                    these very works which I am doing,
             bear me witness that the Father has sent me."

While it is clear that Jesus bears witness to the Father and submits to him, it is also clear that the Father bears witness to the Son and defers to him. The dynamics of the divine Family are relational and symmetrical, as we gather from the following saying in which we read that the Son is sent by the Father and the Father bears witness to the Son and gives him the honor of revealing him in voice and form:

5:37   "And the Father who sent me
                    has himself borne witness to me.
                    His voice you have never heard,
                    his form you have never seen."

In order to recognize that the Son is equal to the Father one must have the internal attesting word of the Father and believe on the Son whom he has sent. Jesus' adversaries have voluntarily rejected the word of both the Father and the Son:

5:38   "And you do not have his word abiding in you,
         for you do not believe him whom he has sent."

Jesus discloses that the Old Testament Scriptures are written about him and thereby makes a radical claim that he is equal with God. It is an astounding thing to say because it implies that the Father and the Spirit, the authors of Scripture, defer to the Son and focus their attention on him. But Jesus' audience has missed the point in their search for truth, like the two who later walked with him on the road to Emmaus, when, "beginning with Moses and all the prophets, he interpreted to them in all the scriptures the things concerning himself" (Luke 24:27):

5:39   "You search the scriptures,
         because you think that in them you have eternal
             life;
         and it is they that bear witness to me."

Eternal life can be obtained only by coming to the Son, who represents the divine Family. Jesus is graciously at the disposal of his hearers, but they will not come to him:

5:40   "Yet you refuse to come to me
         that you may have life."

Jesus declares that his audience does not have the love of God in them and can bring him no glory, implying that his glory comes from the divine Family whose essential nature is love:

5:41   "I do not receive glory from men.
5:42   But I know that you have not the love of God
             within you."

In coming to earth as the incarnate Son Jesus reveals his submission to the Father's will, but at the same time he claims the Father's name and therefore equality with him. The irony of this discourse before an unbelieving audience lies in their refusing to accept him who speaks the truth and comes in the name of the Father; but they will be all too willing to receive someone else who comes in his own name and speaks falsely:

5:43 "I have come in my Father's name,
> and you do not receive me;
> if another comes in his own name,
> him you will receive."

In remonstrating with his unbelieving hearers Jesus makes the claim that he is the glory of God, attesting his equality with God. The reason they reject him is because they are interested only in human glory that is received from one another:

5:44 "How can you believe,
> who receive glory from one another
> and do not seek the glory that comes from the
>   only God?"

Although Jesus has authority to accuse his unbelieving opponents, he does not need to, for the scriptural witness of Moses (cf. 5:39) bears sufficient testimony to the Son's equality with the Father that they stand condemned:

5:45 "Do not think that I shall accuse you to the
>   Father;
> it is Moses who accuses you,
> on whom you set your hope."

Jesus' astounding claim is that Moses and the Old Testament Scriptures refer to him; thus he stands in the very place of God. To believe Moses' testimony is to believe that Jesus is the Son of the Father:

5:46 "If you believed Moses, you would believe me,
> for he wrote of me."

On the other hand, to reject Moses, who writes about God, is to reject Jesus who is equal with God and is therefore the subject of Moses' revelation. Jesus places his words on a par

with the words of God that were spoken by Moses. To disbelieve in the one is to disbelieve in the other:

5:47   "But if you do not believe his writings,
how will you believe my words?"

"I Am the Bread of Life"
Chapter 6

Jesus' notable claim to be coequal with God the Father
continues in his discourse on true bread and drink in
chapter 6. A careful analysis of the passage confirms Jesus'
intention to present himself as the incarnate representative
of the divine Family. He gives warning that his hearers must
not seek the ultimate meaning of food in physical satisfac-
tion (as they have in his feeding of the five thousand, 6:1–
15), but must discover its true origin in his own person as
Son of the Father. By his authoritative manner of speaking a
divine word from the heavenly Family ("Truly, truly, I say to
you"), he invites them to partake of his food as he makes
himself available to them. He bears the seal of the Father
and has authority to bestow the gift of eternal life on behalf
of the divine Community:

6:26   "Truly, truly, I say to you,
you seek me, not because you saw signs,
but because you ate your fill of the loaves.
6:27   Do not labor for the food which perishes,
but for the food which endures to eternal life,
which the Son of man will give to you;
for on him has God the Father set his seal."

Accordingly, Jesus is claiming that as the Son of man he is
equal to God the Father and is the food that endures to
eternal life. The Son of man is the servant who places himself at the disposal of the believer to be eaten, as the Father
places himself at the disposal of the Son in setting his seal of
approval upon him and granting him the distinction of representing the divine Family.

In reply to his listeners' question, "What must we do, to

be doing the work of God?" (6:28), Jesus replies with a challenge that may lead to a situation of genuine disclosure and commitment if they respond to him with belief. They must place themselves at his disposal in order to understand who he is and what his relation to the Father may mean for them. In his reply Jesus makes clear that he is coequal with the Father. To believe in him is to believe in the Father:

6:29   "This is the work of God,
            that you believe in him whom he has sent."

The response of Jesus' audience in asking for a faith sign and work, and their reference to manna in the wilderness (6:30–31), provides opportunity for Jesus to make even more explicit claims about his coequality with the Father, and to tie together Old Testament and new-age images of heavenly food. He is the life-giving bread of God. Son and Father graciously feed their people and make themselves available to them:

6:32   "Truly, truly, I say to you,
            it was not Moses who gave you the bread from
                heaven;
            my Father gives you the true bread from heaven.
6:33   For the bread of God is that which comes down
                from heaven,
            and gives life to the world."

The proper attitude for further disclosure and commitment is openness and deference to the Son who is Lord:

6:34   They said to him,
            "Lord, give us this bread always."

Jesus explicitly defines the bread of 6:32 as himself. It is he who satisfies both hunger and thirst. His use of the authoritative expression *I am* is a claim to be equal with God the "I am" (Exod. 3:14) and gives him the right to offer himself as the means of satisfying hunger and thirst forever. But one must come to him believing in order to receive the gift of eternal life:

6:35   Jesus said to them,
          "I am the bread of life;
            he who comes to me shall not hunger,
            and he who believes in me shall never thirst."

But Jesus observes that they are not coming in the proper attitude of belief. They see him, yet they do not see him. Belief in the Son is necessary to salvation:

6:36   "But I said to you that you have seen me
          and yet do not believe."

Their unbelief does not undo the divine plan of salvation, however. Jesus expresses complete accord with the sovereign will of the Father who will give him those who are to come to faith. Those who come will be received. In the following saying Jesus implicitly claims equality with the Father, for the Father is giving all believers to him; they will come to Jesus, and he will receive them. We note the preponderance of the pronouns *me* and *I* as Jesus claims to act on behalf of the divine Family. The focus is upon the Son as the Father defers to him from the heavenly side and as believers defer to him from the earthly side:

6:37   "All that the Father gives me will come to me;
          and him who comes to me I will not cast out."

Yet as soon as he says that and puts himself forward as the central figure of attention, Jesus characteristically defers to the Father, lest there be any charge that he is putting himself forward at the expense of perfect unity with the Father. Jesus' willingness to be completely at the service of the Father discloses the essential oneness of their relationship:

6:38   "For I have come down from heaven,
          not to do my own will,
          but the will of him who sent me."

The harmonious disposability of Father and Son to the believer, and the Son's equality with the Father, now come into focus again as Jesus promises protection of the believer in the day of resurrection. The relational circle of participation and being there for the other becomes complete as the believer sees the Son, trusts in him, and receives eternal life:

6:39   "And this is the will of him who sent me,
        that I should lose nothing of all that he has
            given me,
        but raise it up at the last day.
6:40   For this is the will of my Father,
        that every one who sees the Son and believes in
            him
          should have eternal life;
        and I will raise him up at the last day."

Jesus' unusual claims arouse murmurings among his hearers because they already know his earthly parents and cannot understand how a human being can claim to be equal with God (6:41–42). The report of their unbelief adds a note of realism to the account and attests its historical accuracy. Jesus makes no apologies and offers no explanations except to continue his self-disclosure in word and deed. He not only restates his claim that he is sent by the Father and has the power to raise up the believer at the last day, but also asserts his unity with the sovereign plan of the Father; only those whom the Father draws to faith will come to Jesus the Son and accept his gracious word on behalf of the divine Family. The Son serves the Father, the Father serves the Son, and together they serve the believer who in turn comes to serve them:

6:43   "Do not murmur among yourselves.
6:44   No one can come to me unless the Father who
        sent me draws him;
        and I will raise him up at the last day."

Jesus claims to fulfill Scripture, specifically Isaiah 54:13, and to identify his instruction with the teaching of the Father, asserting divine coequality:

6:45   "It is written in the prophets,
         'And they shall all be taught by God.'
         Every one who has heard and learned from the
              Father comes to me."

Adding claim to claim Jesus asserts that he is the embodied, visible representative of the Father who alone has seen the Father, implying their equality:

6:46   "Not that any one has seen the Father
         except him who is from God;
         he has seen the Father."

Belief in these truth claims of Jesus about his unity with the Father is the sole means of gaining eternal life. The believer is in effect responding to the gracious availability of Father and Son with a like disposability to the divine Family. Belief in Jesus as representative of the Family brings eternal life as a present possession. To trust in Jesus is to enter the Family circle where eternal life is a present reality:

6:47   "Truly, truly, I say to you,
         he who believes
         has eternal life."

Jesus returns to the theme of food and claims again to be the bread of life (cf. 6:25–35). On human terms it is an incredible assertion because it means that Jesus is naming himself as the source of eternal life and is making himself equal to God. At the same time his simple declaration implies that he is completely at the disposal of the believer, for he is offering himself to be eaten as eternal food:

6:48   "I am the bread of life."

This bare assertion of deity and disposability is further interpreted by Jesus in an antithetic parallelism that begins in verse 49 and is completed in verse 50. Jesus is much more than the manna of the Old Testament, because those who ate

47

that bread died, whereas those who eat of him will never die. Once more he claims to represent the heavenly desire to be graciously available for the believer:

6:49   "Your fathers ate the manna in the wilderness,
            and they died.
6:50   This is the bread which comes down from heaven,
            that a man may eat of it and not die."

Already Jesus has demonstrated his authoritative use of "I am" as an assertion of equality with the Father. Now he asserts the claim once more, but typically not in any sense that serves himself; on the contrary, he makes the claim in order to serve the believer. The generosity of the heavenly Family is expressed in terms of utter disposability to whoever has faith to eat of Jesus. He is completely there for the other:

6:51   "I am the living bread which came down from
            heaven;
            if any one eats of this bread, he will live for
            ever;
            and the bread which I shall give for the life of the
            world
            is my flesh."

In answer to the question of his hearers, "How can this man give us his flesh to eat?" (6:52; cf. Nicodemus' initial query, 3:4), Jesus invites the person of faith to move beyond the image to the original, from the enfleshed Jesus and a literal interpretation of his words to the deeper nature of his person. He is not to be construed merely in physical terms but is to be seen as the Son of man who is there for them, offering his life for their mortal life, and representing the love of the divine Community on their behalf. The Son of man is the Son of God who is standing before them and can be perceived only by the eyes of faith. The divine Family defers to the Son as he offers heavenly grace on their behalf. To believe in him is to eat of him as eternal food; not to believe is not to eat of him who is eternal life. The decision

rests with the hearer, who must place himself at the disposal
of Jesus. There is no other way to gain eternal life. The divine Family has become servant to the fallen creature in
Jesus the Son; now the creature must become servant to the
divine Family through Jesus the Son, believing on him
whom the Father has sent. The negative possibility is expressed first, then the positive:

6:53   "Truly, truly, I say to you,
      unless you eat the flesh of the Son of man
        and drink his blood,
      you have no life in you;
6:54   he who eats my flesh and drinks my blood
      has eternal life,
      and I will raise him up at the last day."

Jesus reasserts the claim with double emphasis: he is indeed *divine* food (that is, he is of God), and he is indeed
divine *food* (that is, he is graciously available to the believer
as the source of eternal life):

6:55   "For my flesh is food indeed,
      and my blood is drink indeed."

Still speaking as the voice of God and as the embodied
expression of the divine Community, Jesus describes the
deeper spiritual meaning of eating his flesh and drinking his
blood. One who has faith in him is drawn into the life of the
divine Family by the mutual indwelling of Son and believer.
This interpersonal communion discloses the essential family
dynamic designed for the re-created human order. The mutual abiding of Jesus and the believer images the interrelationship of the persons of the divine Community:

6:56   "He who eats my flesh and drinks my blood
      abides in me,
      and I in him."

Jesus uses the family analogy in comparing his life with
the Father to his life with the believer. The generosity of the

49

divine Community is evident in the following saying, first concerning Father to Son, then Son to Father, then Son (with Father implied) to believer. Jesus' equality with the Father is implied by his use of the pronoun *me* as object of the believer's worship and source of life. That is balanced by his deference to the Father as the one who has sent him and in whom he lives:

6:57   "As the living Father sent me,
        and I live because of the Father,
     so he who eats me
        will live because of me."

Concluding his address in the synagogue at Capernaum (6:59) Jesus sums up his proclamation by contrasting the old and the new once more. He is far greater than the manna given in the wilderness, for now the bread of heaven has come to earth personally in him, and nourishes to eternal life. Characteristic of his address as a whole, Jesus' summary lays claim to divine status and divine hospitality. Jesus is both God and servant:

6:58   "This is the bread which came down from heaven,
        not such as the fathers ate and died;
    he who eats this bread
        will live for ever."

It is understandable that such outspoken language would offend many of his hearers. It offends many of his disciples, in fact, who "drew back and no longer went about with him" (6:66). Jesus is not discouraged, however, for he affirms again the sovereign will of the Father in the matter of belief and unbelief: "This is why I told you that no one can come to me unless it is granted him by the Father" (6:65). He also asserts his identity with the Father in this choosing: "Did I not choose you, the twelve, and one of you is a devil?" (6:70). The evangelist informs us that "Jesus knew from the first who those were that did not believe, and who it was that should betray him" (6:64). From our exegesis of Jesus' extended address it is clear that he knows who he is and makes confident claims about himself and the Father. It is also clear that his deferential references to the Father, in view of his claim to be equal with him, are meant to be affirmations of oneness with the divine Family that is characterized above all by generosity, disposability, and selfless love. There are clear indications in the teaching of Jesus that the believer is drawn into this Family circle of generosity through faith in the person of the Son. The Father defers to the Son and gives him the honor of representing him, while the Spirit hovers almost anonymously in the background, unmentioned until the close of the discourse, when Jesus refers to the Son of man ascending to heaven, and speaks of the Spirit as life-giving: "It is the spirit that gives life, the flesh is of no avail" (6:63). Accordingly, while the Son fulfills his role as faithful servant to the will of the Father and the Spirit, the Father and the Spirit fulfill their roles as faithful servants to the Son, and all three persons of the Triune Family evince their generous unity in loving service to a fallen creation.

The proper response of believers is to become faithful servants to the divine Family in which they have now been adopted as children. Jesus' dialogues have revealed an essential truth about the Triune God and the creation God has made: self-assertion and individuality are to be defined essentially in terms of interpersonal communion, participation, availability, and love. Ultimately, "feeling at home" is to be at home in the heavenly household which Jesus brings to earth in behalf of the divine Community.

Father, Son, and Spirit,
and the Feast of Tabernacles
Chapter 7

When Jesus goes up privately to the temple at his own appropriate time for the Feast of Tabernacles, and in the middle of the Feast begins to teach in the temple, his response to questions about the source of his learning provides a key to his relationship with the Father. Verse 18 is the core text, but it needs to be seen in the context of the preceding verses. Jesus answers his questioners by renouncing any claim to authority on his own, in complete deference to the authoritative teaching of the Father who has sent him. Indirectly, of course, this amounts to a claim that his teaching and that of the Father are one:

7:16 "My teaching is not mine,
but his who sent me."

Jesus now makes a crucial point in the debate. If anyone chooses to do God's will (as Jesus has), he will know that Jesus does not speak independently of God but in complete accord with him. The implication is that Jesus speaks as the voice of God the Father because he is completely available to him and is there to serve and glorify him. He is totally there for the other. Any flaunting of his own authority is therefore out of the question. For the divine Family, to be is to be there for one another:

7:17 "If any man's will is to do his will,
he shall know whether the teaching is from
God
or whether I am speaking on my own authority."

Jesus' complete availability to the Father is expressed in verse 18. Anyone who tries to speak independently of the Father is by definition self-glorifying and false, like Satan who rebels against the social nature of God and creation and can only destroy (see 8:44). Jesus claims to be speaking the words of the Father not because the incarnation of the Son requires a humanity so empty that he must hear everything from the Father experientially, but because he willingly identifies himself totally with the will of the divine Community. Truth resides only in total unity with the will of that Family. That is the key to Jesus' deferential statements concerning the Father. Accordingly:

7:18 "He who speaks on his own authority
seeks his own glory;
but he who seeks the glory of him who sent him
is true, and in him there is no falsehood."

The saying of 7:18 is therefore a key that unlocks the "hearing" passages. They have nothing to do with his psychological

52

religious development (we have no access to this aspect of his incarnate life), but denote his complete identification with the Father and the absolute truth-speaking of the divine Family, in contrast to those who judge by appearance only rather than with right judgment (7:24). This is borne out by the fact that the Spirit of truth is also described as speaking only what he hears from the Father and the Son. Obviously the Holy Spirit has not undergone psychological religious development. The following saying is fully in accord with the interpretation that the hearing passages resonate with the complete unity of the Triune Family in which there is mutual deference and availability:

16:13 "When the Spirit of truth comes,
　　　　he will guide you into all the truth;
　　　for he will not speak on his own authority,
　　　　but whatever he hears he will speak,
　　　　and he will declare to you the things that are
　　　　　　to come.
16:14 He will glorify me,
　　　　for he will take what is mine and declare it to
　　　　　　you.
16:15 All that the Father has is mine;
　　　　therefore I said that he will take what is mine
　　　　　　and declare it to you."

Accordingly, Jesus can speak in complete unity with the divine Family. In light of 7:18, the following saying suggests that Jesus' total deference and availability to the Father implies his equality with the Father, since the persons of the divine Family equally speak the truth and the Father has deferred to the Son in sending him as spokesman. Jesus makes the candid and truthful judgment that his hearers do not know the Father and therefore miss the meaning of what is happening before their eyes:

7:28 "I have not come of my own accord;
　　　　he who sent me is true,
　　　　　and him you do not know."

Jesus' prophecy of his imminent return to the Father is further evidence of his divine origin. His declaration that his adversaries cannot go where he is going highlights the contrast of 7:28. Jesus knows where his home is and is conscious of his mission to call others home again. His coming and returning imply a unity of purpose and fellowship between Father and Son in the divine Household. The tragedy for his hearers is that in rejecting the Son they reject the Father and the gracious offer of a final homecoming:

7:33   "I shall be with you a little longer,
        and then I go to him who sent me;
7:34   you will seek me and you will not find me;
        where I am you cannot come."

When Jesus' expressions of disposability to the Father are also understood as indirect claims to equality with the Father, there is then no mystery or contradiction in his making direct claims about himself and referring to his own person, for we are to understand that in referring to himself he is doing so in social communion with the Father and the Spirit, signaling the essential unity of the Triune Family. Accordingly, at the end of the Feast Jesus speaks authoritatively for the Family as he offers the spiritually thirsty an invitation to come to him, to believe in him, and to drink of him. These are words spoken by one who is confident of equal status in the divine Family and of bearing the seal of approval of Father and Spirit in speaking the gracious word of salvation on their behalf. As the concluding words of his discourse make clear, Jesus' invitation in his own name is also an invitation in the name of the Spirit, while the Father for the moment is in the background and defers to Son and Spirit. The divine Family is like that, but is always implied when Jesus speaks, simply because it is out of the question for him to act on his own without them. The Triune Family is social to its essential core, hence social in its ministry to a world that is thirsty for hospitality and communion. When the thirsty drink of the Son, the Spirit will make their hearts flow as rivers of living water to others. The image is relational and supremely hospitable:

7:37   "If any one thirst, let him come to me and drink.

7:38   He who believes in me, as the scripture has said,
   'Out of his heart shall flow rivers of living
    water.' "
7:39   Now this he said about the Spirit,
   which those who believed in him were to
    receive;
   for as yet the Spirit had not been given,
    because Jesus was not yet glorified.

As representative of the Triune Family Jesus stands between the times. He fulfills Old Testament images and prophecies about water (e.g., Isa. 12:3; 43:19–20; 44:3; 55:1; 58:11;
Ezek. 47:1–12; Joel 3:18; Zech. 14:8). He fulfills the meaning
of the Feast of Tabernacles (Lev. 23:33–43; Ps. 118:24–27;
Isa. 12:3) and is the true water (John 4:10). But he also
prophesies that his work will continue with the outpouring
of the Spirit in the time to come. He makes notable claims
about his person and work, yet in the next breath defers to
Father and Spirit.

This paradox affords an innermost clue to the nature of
the Triune Family and we shall see it appearing in every
address of Jesus throughout the Gospel.

3

The Family of Father and Son
John 8–12

The interpersonal communion of Father and Son and the alternation between Jesus' affirmation of this communion and his bold declaration of "I am" is given articulate expression in the sayings recorded in chapters 8–12. Light, freedom, and glory are among the central metaphors by which Jesus describes his ministry to the world on behalf of the divine Family.

The "I Am" Claims of Jesus
Chapter 8

Jesus' authoritative use of the personal pronoun *I* focuses attention on himself and his ministry to those in darkness. His claim to be the light of the world needs to be seen in context of his complementary sayings about the Father made elsewhere in the chapter. Side by side lie statements that claim equality with God and affirmations that intimate complete transparency to the Father. Jesus begins with a dramatic claim that he personally embodies the light and life of God. At the same time it is clear that his claim is an act of charity because he is lending himself to whoever will accept his gracious hospitality:

8:12   "I am the light of the world;
         he who follows me will not walk in darkness,
         but will have the light of life."

The dramatic contrast between Jesus and his adversaries is given ironical expression in their ungenerous response, which disregards Jesus' earlier declaration that he is seeking the glory of God and that in him there is no falsehood (7:18):

8:13   "You are bearing witness to yourself;
         your testimony is not true."

Jesus' reply to this charge helps the hearer perceive that while Jesus is indeed bearing witness to himself he is not putting himself forward at the expense of the Family he represents. On the contrary, it is because the divine Community has honored the Son as embodied spokesman that he can speak in terms of himself. Whether Jesus' audience understands his heavenly origin and destination determines how his words about himself will be taken. He knows where he has come from and where he is going and can speak openly about himself, knowing that the Father and the Spirit are with him and have deferred to him as their voice. Lacking faith and generosity, his opponents misconstrue his remarks and entirely miss the significance of his person and his mission. They have no grasp of the higher reality but judge according to their fallen sense of what Jesus' personal reference actually means. Because they are essentially selfish they assume that his use of the personal *I* is likewise selfish. Jesus contradicts their misinterpretation by challenging their theological assumptions, while affirming the truth of his own interpretation of the real situation:

8:14   "Even if I do bear witness to myself, my testimony
                is true,
             for I know whence I have come and whither I
                am going,
              but you do not know whence I have come
                or whither I am going."

Jesus continues his attack on the falsehood of his adversaries that would repudiate his status as spokesman for the divine Family. They judge falsely because they judge by appearances according to the flesh (*kata tēn sarka*), while Jesus judges no one falsely because he judges in unity with the Father:

8:15   "You judge according to the flesh,
                I judge no one.
8:16   "Yet even if I do judge,
                my judgment is true,
             for it is not I alone that judge,
                but I and he who sent me."

Jesus now reveals something quite remarkable about himself and the Father. He repeatedly expresses that he is at the disposal of the Father and bears witness to him; but now he says that the relationship is mutual and symmetrical: the Father is also at the disposal of the Son and bears witness to him. The Family of God exemplifies its own divinely revealed law by sustaining testimony by multiple witnesses. The Son bears witness to himself and the Father sustains that witness. The divine Family quotes its own law concerning truthfulness, and lives by it:

8:17   "In your law it is written
            that the testimony of two men is true;
8:18   I bear witness to myself,
            and the Father who sent me bears witness to
                me."

Jesus' opponents press the question from unbelief, "Where is your Father?" (8:19), and he replies with an equation that clearly links his own person indissolubly with the Father. Not only are Jesus the Son and the Father coequal, but also from the human point of view the Father can be known only through the Son. The beginning of wisdom is to know the Son who introduces the believer to the Father. It is a striking claim:

8:19   "You know neither me
            nor my Father;
        if you knew me,
            you would know my Father also."

Jesus continues his address to an unbelieving audience, declaring the necessity of seeing the incarnate Son in the lower realm of the world as revealer of the Father in the higher realm. It is not possible for those in the lower realm of the fallen world to know the truth except by believing that Jesus is from above. He is conscious of being from the higher world and of having come to redeem the sinful world. The unbelief of the world leads to death. Only belief in Jesus the Son leads to life:

8:23 "You are from below,
   I am from above;
 you are of this world,
   I am not of this world.
8:24 I told you that you would die in your sins,
   for you will die in your sins
   unless you believe that I am he."

They persist in their unbelief. "Who are you?" they ask
(8:25). In reply Jesus gives no evidence of groping for an
answer as though he had to learn from the Father who he is
through a developing religious consciousness. He has known
and proclaimed his sonship from the beginning of his ministry; hence he can reply:

8:25 "Even what I have told you
   from the beginning."

A further example of Jesus' dual role as both submissive
and self-assertive member of the divine Community is to be
found in the following passage. After speaking directly of
himself as the center of revelation and redemption, he proceeds to give all glory to the Father in selfless admiration. At
the same time he attests his interpersonal communion and
unity with the Father:

8:26 "I have much to say about you and much to
      judge;
   but he who sent me is true,
 and I declare to the world
   what I have heard from him."

Since his hearers do not understand that he is speaking of
the Father (8:27), he utters a prophecy concerning the com-
prehension that will follow his death. At that time they will
understand Jesus' complete faithfulness, availability, and
submission to the Father, and his desire to claim nothing on
his own apart from the Family relationship. That he does
nothing on his own authority but speaks only as the Father
has taught him does not describe the human process of his

learning but is a typical figure of speech Jesus employs to describe his utter love and servanthood and his total unity with the thought of the Father. Nothing extraneous or selfish intrudes itself upon the perfect accord of the divine Society:

8:28   "When you have lifted up the Son of man,
        then you will know that I am he,
    and that I do nothing on my own authority
        but speak thus as the Father taught me."

This radical saying is immediately complemented by an intimation that he and the Father are one, for the Father is with him and has not left him alone. The key to understanding Jesus' statements of subordination to the Father is to be found in the second half of verse 29. It is also the key to the essential motivation of the persons of the Triune Community and their interpersonal communion. It it always to do what is pleasing to one another:

8:29   "And he who sent me is with me;
        he has not left me alone,
        for I always do what is pleasing to him."

To be completely available, to rally and lend oneself to the other, to give the gift of self, to admire with constancy and fidelity, to be responsive and porous and to belong to the other, these qualities mark the real person. That is what Jesus is saying of himself in his relationship to the Father, and it is what he is saying of the divine Society as a whole. Each of the persons of the Community is for the other, wholly consecrated to doing what is pleasing to one another.

Jesus' testimony is initially effective, for many believe in him as he testifies in this vein, and to them he speaks a similar word of availability that reflects the interpersonal love of the divine Family (8:30–31). He calls upon them to place themselves at his disposal by continuing in his word and discovering the truth that will make them free (8:31–32). When Jesus speaks to them of freedom, however, they resist going any further with his teaching because they con-

61

sider themselves already free by heritage in their father Abraham. They have never been in bondage and resent his intimation that they are not really free (8:33). But Jesus strongly asserts the superiority of his Father over Abraham and his oneness with the Father, thus his authority to offer them true freedom. In seeking to kill him they reveal themselves to be slaves to sin and sons of another father, the devil (8:34–38). In the middle of this heightening controversy, in which each party accuses the other of being satanic and claims true spiritual fatherhood, Jesus makes the singular announcement that the truth that will make them free (8:32) is none other than himself:

8:36   "So if the Son makes you free,
             you will be free indeed."

But he frames this declaration of himself as personified truth and freedom with the claim that he has seen (8:38) and heard (8:40) this from God the Father, implying that he is the duly appointed spokesman for the divine Community. Although they claim to have "one Father, even God" (8:41), Jesus falsifies their claim and logic by pointing out that if they truly had God as their Father they would accept him as the Son. He strongly asserts his deity in the face of their unbelief and implies that he is equal with God and equally worthy of love, because he proceeds and comes from God:

8:42   "If God were your Father,
             you would love me,
             for I proceeded and came forth from God."

Yet as soon as he says that and directs attention to himself, he defers to the Father and gives him pride of place. The duality of self-affirmation and deference in Jesus' ministry is again stated in this remark:

8:42   "I came not of my own accord,
             but he sent me."

Jesus now returns to the pole of self-affirmation, employing the personal pronouns *I* and *me* as his focus of authority. It is because "you do not understand what I say," are not able to bear "to hear my word," that "you do not believe me" (8:43, 45), he says to them, accusing them of satanic and murderous intent and false speech (8:44). The accusation that they are speaking lies that lead to murder, in imitation of the devil, accords with our remarks in chapter 1 that at the heart of God's social covenant is the gift of language. Where this is honored there is life and freedom; where it is abused there is slavery and death. Rejecting the invitation to life that the Son of the Family offers them, they choose to believe the lie of the father of lies and accuse Jesus of demon possession and of being a Samaritan (8:45–48), a double insult on their terms.

Jesus overlooks the slur about being a Samaritan, having already found more belief among the Samaritans than among his own (chap. 4), but the accusation that he is demon possessed is another matter. That is a direct and ultimate attack on his credentials and the divine Community. They dishonor the Son and the Father, while Jesus' principal aim is to honor the Father. Their accusation demands a stern response, and Jesus expresses it in terms of honor, implying that they are the ones who are demon possessed, and so dishonor the divine Family (their blasphemy against Father and Son also implies a blasphemy against the Holy Spirit; see Matt. 12:22–32):

8:49   "I have not a demon;
           but I honor my Father,
               and you dishonor me."

The intercommunion of Father and Son and their sole desire to glorify and give pleasure to one another (cf. 8:29) are articulated in Jesus' following word. He first shifts focus from himself to the Father, whereupon the Father refocuses attention on the Son and vindicates him. There is a divine altruism that defines the life of the divine Community:

8:50 "Yet I do not seek my own glory:
there is One who seeks it
and he will be the judge."

In the intimate relationship between Father and Son the Father's word is the Son's word, and the Son's word is the Father's word. If a believer keeps the Son's word and honors the gift of faithful speech that Jesus embodies, he will eternally enjoy the fellowship of the divine Family. This is implied in Jesus' next utterance where again he does not hesitate to speak of himself as the object of the believer's obedience and faithfulness:

8:51 "Truly, truly, I say to you,
if any one keeps my word,
he will never see death."

In this saying Jesus equates himself with God the Father, the source of life. His hearers understand the equation but reject its truth, accusing him again of having a demon and of making himself greater than mortal Abraham (8:52–53). To their renewed attack on the truthfulness of his claim Jesus replies once again by deflecting attention from himself to the Father, who in turn deflects attention from himself to the Son. Jesus denies that he means to glorify himself, for this would be contrary to the nature of the divine Family; but he does not hesitate to claim that the Father glorifies him. Each person of the divine Community admires the other, rallies to and affirms the other, communes in divine hospitality with the other, seeks only to please the other. This divine disposability reflects the essential oneness of the First Family. Jesus divests himself of self-seeking and defers to the Father, but then claims that the Father glorifies him. The failure of Jesus' audience to understand this truth brings into question the genuineness of their faith in God and whether they have known him at all:

8:54 "If I glorify myself,
my glory is nothing;
it is my Father
who glorifies me,
of whom you say that he is your God."

Jesus now makes two bold statements, one a declaration that in fact they have not and do not know the Father because they reject the Son, and the other an affirmation that he knows the Father, is the fulfillment of the eschatological day Abraham rejoiced to see, and is conscious of having existed before Abraham. As to the first, Jesus declares that he must speak the truth, and the truth is that he knows God and keeps his word because, by implication, he is one with God in the divine Society. Their denial of this fact reveals only that their posture is one of falsehood and unreality, for they have repudiated the true social nature of reality by repudiating the Son who speaks for the ultimate social Family. They do not "know" God as true children of the Family should give evidence of knowing God; but Jesus does know God because he is the Son of the Father and evinces the essential Family quality of loving availability and interpersonal communion, whereas they do not:

8:55　"But you have not known him;
　　　I know him.
　　　If I said, I do not know him,
　　　　I should be a liar like you;
　　　but I do know him
　　　　and I keep his word."

Jesus concludes his declamation by making the outlandish (to their ears) claim that not only is he the historical embodiment of Abraham's prophetic vision (8:56), but actually predates Abraham altogether (8:58). The first wins his audience's incredulity, the second their fury and intent to put him to death (8:59):

8:58　"Truly, truly, I say to you,
　　　before Abraham was,
　　　　I am."

Jesus' claim to knowledge of his preexistence as the "I am" (tantamount to claiming equality with God) constitutes a challenge to the interpreter of this Gospel. If the incarnation theme of 1:14 is taken seriously there is no problem, for one would expect that the Word who was with God and was God (1:1) would speak in this fashion when he became embodied in space and time. If the saying of 8:58 is taken to be a later redaction of the church and a meditation on the significance of Christ, then the motif of 1:14 would have to be qualified and the high claims of Jesus interpreted docetically. This would make the Gospel an early example of gnostic thought, where true incarnation is denied and revelation is confined to esoteric knowledge designed for the few (contrary to the stated theme of 20:31: "but these are written that you may believe that Jesus is the Christ, the Son of God, and that believing you may have life in his name"). The weight of the Gospel is against such an interpretation, as is the synoptic tradition (which will be examined in another volume). The claim of 8:58 could not be denied without bringing into question the other claims of Jesus that he is equal with God. This declaration by Jesus affirms that he is conscious of being the personal incarnation of the preexistent Word in history and that as God the Son he has come in human flesh as representative of the divine Community.

The violent reaction to Jesus' remarks highlights the irony of the situation. Jesus claims to have spoken truthfully of his relationship to the divine Society, and his opponents label his claim false. But he labels false their understanding of what the oneness of God (Deut. 6:4) really implies. It does not mean that God is only one person, for that would deny that the Father and the Son (and the Spirit) comprise a divine Family. Jesus is implying that the traditional Mosaic revelation that God is one describes the essential unity of God, and that the further revelation he is making as Son of God discloses the essential sociality of God as divine Community. Thus they are using a partial revelation made by God himself in an earlier epoch as an argument against God's further disclosure of his true nature. The incident is charged with irony, for their monotheistic faith is brought to fulfillment only in the Father's generous gift of the Son in whom alone, Jesus is saying, there is life and salvation and incorporation into the Community as children of God.

"I Am the Light of the World"
Chapter 9

In healing the man born blind Jesus follows the pattern
that has typified his ministry to this point, affirming on
the one hand his personal authority and on the other his
role as representative of the divine Family. As he prepares
to heal the blind man he alludes to his unity with God
and at the same time claims that he himself is the light of
the world who brings sight where there is darkness. Suffering becomes a challenge and an opportunity for Jesus to
manifest the works of God and to make a compound good
out of a hitherto unmitigated evil. In answer to his disciples' question as to who had sinned, the man or his
parents, that this person has suffered from blindness, Jesus
does not look back at behavioral factors that determine
evil but forward to the release of power that will bring
this lost soul to see the physical world, and more impor-
tantly, the spiritual world Jesus embodies in his own person. Jesus first speaks of God's works, placing himself
momentarily in the background:

9:3   "It was not that this man sinned,
                or his parents,
            but that the works of God
                might be made manifest in him."

Although the sick man is in physical darkness and Jesus' critics are in spiritual darkness, the irony is that it is
now daytime when the works of God are being manifest.
Soon it will be night again when no one can do such
works of healing, but the present is the eschatological day
when the divine Community is working at the disposal of
a world in darkness. Jesus shows deference to the Father
as the one who has sent him and implies his equality with
the Father as spokesman for the divine Family. He also
implies that his is a social ministry in two respects: the
divine Community is at work, and Jesus' followers are
working with him as the nucleus of a new community;
hence the plural *we:*

9:4   "We must work the works of him who sent me,
        while it is day;
        night comes,
           when no one can work."

Having kept himself in the background to this point, Jesus now focuses attention on himself as the personal embodiment of light to a dark world, indicating that it is perfectly natural for him to move back and forth from self-forgetfulness to self-affirmation. Yet it is not for personal glory that he speaks the authoritative "I am," but for the benefit of the world that is in darkness. As the "I am" Jesus represents the divine Society that is at the disposal of the dark world:

9:5   "As long as I am in the world,
       I am the light of the world."

A heated controversy follows Jesus' healing of the blind man, since the healing takes place on the sabbath when no work is to be done ("This man is not from God, for he does not keep the sabbath" [9:16]). Others overlook the infraction and view the healing on a higher level ("How can a man who is a sinner do such signs?" [9:16]). The scene is fraught with irony that is increased by the simple testimony of the healed man ("Whether he is a sinner, I do not know; one thing I know, that though I was blind, now I see" [9:25]). The experience of healing cannot be contradicted except by insisting on rules that fly in the face of evidence. The healed man accepts the evidence and begins to see spiritually; Jesus' critics reject the evidence and miss the real meaning of Moses and Jesus ("We know that God has spoken to Moses, but as for this man, we do not know where he comes from" [9:29]). They also reject the spoken testimony of the healed man and play the game strictly according to the rules: "You were born in utter sin, and would you teach us?" (9:34).

The prideful blindness of the religious authorities heightens the irony of the incident. Jesus will shortly make a comment on the twofold nature of his ministry that brings blessing to the open and judgment to the hardened, but for the present he continues his work of healing in the life of the man born blind and presses him for a commitment that will enable him to see spiritually. Responding in faith to Jesus' declaration that he is the Son of man in whom one must believe, the man makes himself wholly available to Jesus by responding, "Lord, I believe" (9:35–38). Jesus does not discourage this act of belief in himself but encourages it, confirming that he is conscious of representing the divine Community in its work of bringing light to the world.

The healing episode concludes with Jesus' declaration of a twofold ministry. He claims to bring the world under the light of divine judgment, judging, paradoxically, that repentant sinners may see and that unrepentant sinners may become blind:

9:39   "For judgment I came into this world,
           that those who do not see may see,
           and that those who see may become blind."

Accordingly, while the story begins with Jesus referring to the works of God (9:3), it is evident that he is the one who has been given the honor of doing the works of the divine Family on behalf of a world lost in darkness. His ministry is characterized by availability as he offers the light of divine grace to the blind, but he must also be met by availability on the part of the hearer. If he is, the hearer will see; if he is not, the listener will become blind, even if he thinks he can see. The story related in chapter 9 demonstrates that Jesus intends to draw those who are lost in darkness into a fellowship of light with the divine Community, where all are at the disposal of one another in hospitality and communion.

The Shepherd and His Flock: A Social Image
Chapter 10

Moving from the dynamic and tense episode of the healing of the blind man, the evangelist turns in chapter 10 to Jesus' description of himself as the good shepherd and his teaching on the right and false ways of entering the sheepfold (10:1–18). The contrast flows naturally from the theme in chapter 9 of two kinds of hearers and again leads to a division in Jesus' audience (10:19–21). The second section of the chapter records a parallel episode in which Jesus' claim to be coequal with God is met by increasing hostility, although some believe (10:22–42).

The first section of the chapter describes how Jesus distinguishes between the thief and the robber who climbs into the sheepfold by another way than through the door and the shepherd who enters in at the door, knows the gatekeeper, knows the sheep by name, leads them out, and has their confidence (10:1–5). As this figure of speech is unclear to his audience, Jesus speaks more explicitly and authoritatively of his own person (10:6–18). In this declaration of his redemptive mission Jesus makes his personal claims of equality with the Father plain enough that a response has to be made either to affirm or reject him. He focuses attention on himself as the "I am" and stands in the very place of God himself as door and shepherd of salvation, claiming that the figures of speech applied to God in the Old Testament (e.g., Ps. 23; Jer. 23; Ezek. 34) are fulfilled in him. At the same time he continues the judgment motif of chapter 9 and attacks the false shepherding of the religious authorities who oppose him. Jesus' description of the door as gateway to the sheep's safety is a social metaphor and describes his role as the opening by which oneness of flock and family is realized. The sheep, who represent the believing family, have the gift of discernment to know who is charitably disposed to the family and will provide salvation and freedom of access. Jesus asserts that he is the savior of the flock, assuming the place of God and placing himself at the disposal of the sheep that they may feed abundantly:

10:7　"Truly, truly, I say to you,
　　　I am the door of the sheep.

10:8　All who came before me are thieves and robbers;
　　　but the sheep did not heed them.

10:9　I am the door;
　　　if any one enters by me,
　　　　he will be saved,
　　　　and will go in and out and find pasture."

While Jesus' motivation is hospitable and charitable and transparent to the gracious availability of the divine Community, the thief is arrogant, selfish, and destructive and works against the social unity of the flock for his own advantage. The contrast between destructive malevolence and creative benevolence is highlighted by Jesus in the following antithetic parallel:

10:10 "The thief comes only to steal
            and kill and destroy;
        I came that they may have life,
            and have it abundantly."

Jesus now offers himself as the shepherd of Ezekiel 34 ("I myself will be the shepherd of my sheep" [Ezek. 34:15]) and assumes the very role of God himself. Moreover, he fulfills the role of the Davidic servant-messiah ("And I will set up over them one shepherd, my servant David, and he shall feed them: he shall feed them and be their shepherd" [Ezek. 34:23]), thereby combining in his affirmation claims both to deity and to servanthood. His radical generosity to the sheep in laying down his life is a veiled prophecy of his coming death on behalf of the community and denotes his willingness to be utterly at the disposal of his people. He makes the ultimate declaration of divine disposability when he says:

10:11 "I am the good shepherd.
        The good shepherd lays down his life
            for the sheep."

Jesus contrasts himself with the hireling who thinks only of himself because he does not own the sheep, has no lasting commitment to the sheep, and deserts them when the wolf comes, causing them to be scattered and destroyed. The hireling does not participate in the life of the flock nor does he truly care about them; accordingly he is not really available or accessible to their needs. He is not at their disposal because he is not a member of the family:

10:12 "He who is a hireling and not a shepherd,
        whose own the sheep are not,

71

> sees the wolf coming and leaves the sheep and
>> flees;
> and the wolf snatches them and scatters them.
>
> **10:13** He flees because he is a hireling
> and cares nothing for the sheep."

On the other hand, Jesus describes his relationship to the sheep in terms of an intercommunion that reflects the intercommunion of Father and Son. As the persons of the divine Family are essentially social and available to one another in love and fidelity, so are Shepherd and sheep, Son and believers. Jesus loves his sheep with a love that mirrors the Father's love for him, and reciprocally as the Son loves the Father so the sheep love the Shepherd. Mutual knowledge (= love) originates in the divine Community and is reflected in the redeemed community, Jesus being the key figure who brings the two realms together in interpersonal communion. Through him the divine Family begets a redeemed created family; but the cost is high, requiring the death of the Shepherd on behalf of the sheep:

> **10:14** "I am the good shepherd;
> I know my own and my own know me,
>
> **10:15** as the Father knows me and I know the Father;
> and I lay down my life for the sheep."

Jesus unveils the extent of his social mission by speaking of an expanded family of sheep beyond the present fold, signifying the worldwide scope of his ministry. His authoritative use of "I" and "my voice" implies his consciousness of equality with the Father and of speaking in behalf of the divine Family. The one-and-many theme is also reiterated; as oneness characterizes the Community of God, so oneness is imaged in the community of one flock under one shepherd:

> **10:16** "And I have other sheep,
> that are not of this fold;
> I must bring them also,
> and they will heed my voice.
> So there shall be one flock,
> one shepherd."

That the Father loves the Son is evident from Jesus' previous discourse, but that the Father loves the Son because he lays down his life one might not have guessed. Jesus says that the love that exists between Father and Son lies in a willingness to be utterly at the disposal of the other. This implies not only the mutual disposability of Son to Father and Father to Son, but of Father and Son to the world. The gift of self, of lending oneself in radical humility, is the key to life within both the divine Community and the redeemed community. The humble descent of the Shepherd in laying down his life for the sheep culminates in his resurrection and life for the flock. The way up is the way down in sacrificial servanthood:

10:17 "For this reason the Father loves me,
    because I lay down my life,
    that I may take it again."

That Jesus is conscious of oneness with the Father in representing the gracious availability of the divine Community, and that he is conscious of having at his hand divine power to lay down his life and to take it again, is evident in his concluding remark to his audience. Jesus' sovereign power over his destiny and his voluntary generosity attest his equality with the Father as well as his generosity to the faithful in death and resurrection. Yet the Son's claim to power and authority is complemented by a final word of deference to the Father, for Jesus is not selfishly executing his own will but expressing the will of the Father, voicing the unified will of the divine Family who defer to one another by nature and generously place themselves sympathetically at the disposal of a fallen world, that it might be brought into family unity:

10:18 "No one takes it from me,
    but I lay it down of my own accord.
  I have power to lay it down,
    and I have power to take it again;
  this charge I have received from my Father."

Jesus' proclamation elicits the same kind of mixed response from his hearers as before (9:16), some rejecting,
some still pondering the power of his miracle in healing the
blind man (10:19–21). They demand more evidence, com-
plaining that he has not spoken clearly enough and is baf-
fling them ("How long will you keep us in suspense? If you
are the Christ, tell us plainly" [10:24]). His rebuttal is scath-
ing in its judgment of their unbelief: they are not of his
sheep, they do not hear his voice nor do they follow him. Yet
his works are sufficiently clear so that they are without excuse. They must believe in order to see the working of Father
and Son; if they do not believe, they incur the judgment of
the divine Society whom they are rejecting. The coequality
of Father and Son is tersely expressed in this saying, as Jesus
works in the Father's name and the Father, implied, bears
witness through these works to the Son:

10:25   "I told you, and you do not believe.
The works that I do in my Father's name,
they bear witness to me."

Jesus' unbelieving critics are now told face to face that
they do not believe because they do not belong to the redeemed community. Jesus speaks in the place of God, discerning who are and are not members of the family he has
come to gather:

10:26   "But you do not believe,
because you do not belong to my sheep."

The criterion for distinguishing between sheep and non-
sheep is reciprocal availability and interpersonal communion, where each party is transparent and hospitable to the
other. Believers who comprise the flock are consecrated to
and immersed in the Shepherd and recognize his voice and
respond to him by placing themselves at his disposal, as he
has placed himself at their disposal by shepherding them
and laying down his life for them. As Father and Son reciprocate in interpersonal communion and listen to one
another's voice in a manner befitting the divine Family, so

the reflected redeemed family respond to the servant Shepherd by rallying to his call in a manner befitting those who are "at home" in Jesus:

10:27   "My sheep hear my voice,
and I know them,
and they follow me."

That the believing sheep are eternally at home in the Shepherd is clear from the following words from Jesus. His adversaries pose a threat to the security of his flock, but he pronounces them safe by a sovereign word, expressing his generosity as the one who exercises the divine right to grant eternal life. Jesus asserts his authority and focuses attention on himself through his use of the personal pronouns *I* and *my:*

10:28   "And I give them eternal life,
and they shall never perish,
and no one shall snatch them out of my hand."

Yet Jesus no sooner asserts his divine power than he immediately glorifies the Father as greater than all, typically deferring to the Father by the charitable formula of the Family. In 10:28 it is Jesus who protects the sheep, here in verse 29 the Father. Coequality and deference are in equilibrium when the two statements are taken side by side. The protecting hand of the Son is one with the protecting hand of the Father:

10:29   "My Father, who has given them to me,
is greater than all,
and no one is able to snatch them
out of the Father's hand."

The progression of Jesus' declamation is clear to the discerning eye. Father defers to the Son, Son defers to the Father, and both are absolutely one, not only in their interpersonal communion as divine Family but also in their gracious disposability on behalf of the sheep who constitute the redeemed family. The climax is unequivocal in its declaration of the permeability, porosity, mutual accessibility, and unity of the divine Community:

10:30 "I and the Father are one."

The effect of this declaration on Jesus' unbelieving hearers is predictable in light of a traditional reading of Deuteronomic monotheism (Deut. 6:4). They take up stones to stone him (10:31) because he appears guilty of blasphemy, but Jesus challenges their verdict by bringing to bear the evidence of good works which the Father has worked through him. The equation of Jesus' "I" with the Father, as together they manifest the good works that represent the generous love of the divine Family, testifies to Jesus' oneness with the Father, the unity of the Family, and its generosity to believers. On what basis then will Jesus' adversaries use monotheistic theology to gainsay evidence that God is not only one but also a divine Family characterized by the generous hospitality and love of Father and Son in concert?

10:32 "I have shown you many good works
from the Father;
for which of these
do you stone me?"

The charge is blasphemy: "We stone you for no good work but for blasphemy; because you, being a man, make yourself God" (10:33; cf. 5:18; Lev. 24:16). Their assumption is that Jesus is only a man, denying his witness that he is the Son of God in human flesh who speaks and acts not merely as a prophet for the Father but as the Father himself. Jesus quotes from authoritative Scripture, Psalm 82:6, and employs the subtle argument that if the judges of Israel could be called "gods, sons of the Most High" because of their office, even though they judged unjustly and will themselves be judged (Ps. 82:2, 7), how much more should he be called Son by the Father, since he is wholly just and is truly one with the Father. It therefore follows that Jesus, knowing that he is consecrated and sent into the world by the Father to speak on behalf of the Father, cannot be accused of blasphemy because he calls himself the Son of God and claims equality with God:

10:34   "Is it not written in your law,
       'I said, you are gods'?
10:35   If he called them gods
       to whom the word of God came
       (and scripture cannot be broken),
10:36   do you say of him whom the Father consecrated
       and sent into the world,
       'You are blaspheming,'
     because I said,
       'I am the Son of God'?"

On the basis of this logical argument Jesus presents a rhetorical challenge to his opponents. They need not believe in him if his works are not the works of the Father. But then they must appeal to the Father himself in order to define what good works are. Once they do they cannot deny that the works Jesus is doing are consonant with the works the Father would do. There is then no logic in denying that the works of the Son are the works of the Father because Father and Son participate in each other as one. Jesus' confrontation concludes with a statement of unity with the Father as he attests the presence of the divine Family in his spoken and acted language, indeed in his person. This "inness" theme, explicitly stated here, is novel, astonishing, and climactic:

10:37   "If I am not doing the works of my Father,
       then do not believe me;
10:38   but if I do them,
       even though you do not believe me,
         believe the works,
     that you may know and understand
       that the Father is in me
       and I am in the Father."

The episode concludes with their rejection of Jesus' invitation and their attempt to arrest him (10:39). This continues the tension that has been building up between his drawing the lost and the sick into a redeemed community and his opponents' rejection on doctrinal grounds of his clarification of Mosaic monotheism in terms of a divine Community. On the positive side, the evangelist notes at the close of the account that many came and believed in him when he withdrew across the Jordan, at the place where John the Baptist had earlier borne witness to Jesus (10:40–42).

"I Am the Resurrection and the Life"
Chapter 11

The story of Lazarus' death and resurrection occupies a central position spatially in the Gospel of John and anticipates the death and resurrection of Jesus at the end of the account. It is likely that the evangelist also views the episode involving Lazarus as theologically central in the unfolding of Jesus' ministry and gives it pride of place in the middle of the Gospel as a thematic climax to part 1 of Jesus' work, followed by part 2 which runs parallel on a higher level and climaxes with the death and resurrection of Jesus himself. Whatever we may make of this parallel arrangement, it is clear, from evidence already cited and to be given that Jesus evinces both his human and divine natures in one person as he represents the gracious disposability of the divine Society on behalf of the bereaved and the dead, and works a miracle to restore a family broken by the effects of death.

Jesus seems to see with positive and redemptive vision into events that appear in the outer realm to be heavy with tragedy. As with the man born blind, whose healing is an opportunity for the glorification of Father and Son (9:3–5), so here in explicit terms Jesus views the illness of Lazarus as an opportunity for the mutual glorification of Father and Son. He consciously speaks as the Son of God and implies coequality with the Father:

11:4   "This illness is not unto death;
it is for the glory of God,
so that the Son of God may be glorified by
means of it."

78

Jesus identifies himself with resurrection and life and uses the personal pronouns *I* and *me* as unmistakable clues to his sense of identification with God the Father who is the source of life. His invitation to belief in himself, and his implicit claim that this is wholly legitimate, bears evidence that he is conscious of speaking in behalf of the divine Society. He replies to Martha:

11:25 "I am the resurrection and the life;
      he who believes in me, though he die,
         yet shall he live,
11:26 and whoever lives and believes in me
      shall never die.
Do you believe this?"

Martha's positive reply makes her available to further revelation of Jesus' power over life and death ("Yes, Lord; I believe that you are the Christ, the Son of God, he who is coming into the world" [11:27]). Later at the high point of the episode, as Jesus is about to bring forth Lazarus from the dead, he again replies to Martha about the importance of belief. Belief is necessary if one is to see beyond the outer appearances of events to their inner reality. The glory of God is about to be revealed in the reversal of the curse of death and decay:

11:40 "Did I not tell you that if you would believe
      you would see the glory of God?"

As the stone is removed from the tomb Jesus prays to the Father, expressing both confidence in his shared power in the divine Family and his desire that those standing by might believe in his mission. We infer from Jesus' prayer that the Father listens always to the Son and defers to him, that Father and Son are mutually available to one another, and that both are at the disposal of the world:

11:41 "Father, I thank thee that thou hast heard me.
11:42 I knew that thou hearest me always,
      but I have said this on account of the people
         standing by,
      that they may believe that thou didst send me."

The suggestion that Jesus' listening to the Father might refer to his personal religious experience as the Father progressively teaches him would need to be scrutinized in light of Jesus' claim that the Father always listens to him. Listening and hearing are figures of speech that imply availability, disposability, and being there for the other. What is interesting about the passage (11:41–42) is that the Father also hears: he hears the Son and is always available to do the will of the Son. All three persons of the Triune Society hear one another and do one another's bidding, including the Spirit of truth who listens to the Son and the Father and speaks what he hears (16:13–15). In the divine Community all are mutually equal and mutually subordinate because their nature is always to be there for one another. According to Jesus' own explanation of his prayer, he prays not for his own benefit (he knows the Father always hears him), but for the benefit of those present in order that they might believe in the redeeming work of the divine Family.

"If Any One Serves Me, the Father Will Honor Him"
Chapter 12

As the ministry of Jesus moves to its fulfillment, and as those who hear and observe him divide increasingly into two camps, he speaks more intensely of his coming suffering and the necessity of his followers serving him faithfully. The sequel to the healing of Lazarus and his family circle takes place at Bethany where Mary prophetically anticipates the burial of Jesus in her humble act of disposability as she anoints his feet with costly ointment (12:1–8; cf. Matt. 26:6–13; Mark 14:3–9, which are complementary accounts of the event). As the death of Lazarus and his resurrection have brought a small circle of family and friends together in closer fellowship, so the costly death of Jesus will draw a larger family into fellowship with the divine Family. This is followed by an account of Jesus' entry into Jerusalem (12:12–19) where the Lazarus motif continues as "the crowd that had been with him when he called Lazarus out of the tomb and raised him from the dead bore witness" (12:17). Their prophetic witness to Jesus as the King of Israel who comes in the name of the Lord (12:13) and his entry into Jerusalem on a young ass (12:14) is later understood by the disciples, after Jesus' glorification, to be a fulfillment of Old Testament prophecy (12:16; Zech. 9:9). Jesus' entry into Jerusalem is an acted parable that serves as the point of transition from Act 1 to Act 2 of the drama the divine Community is working out through the Son. The ironic theme of death preceding life is articulated at a deeper level as Jesus now expounds upon the cost of divine hospitality.

The fruitfulness that will result from his coming death and the faithfulness that will be required of his followers are intimated by Jesus in his answer to Philip and Andrew. Jesus views this paradoxically as the hour of glorification and humiliation. He speaks first of glorification, of his own glory as the Son. The implication is that the Father will glorify the Son and defer in his honor:

12:23 "The hour has come for the Son of man
to be glorified."

Yet as soon as he speaks of glorification Jesus complements the glory with suffering, for the path upward is preceded by the path downward. Jesus' conviction that his death will be the seed which will bear the fruit of many believers reflects the desire of the divine Community to be at the disposal of the lost, including the Gentiles whom Philip and Andrew represent:

12:24 "Truly, truly, I say to you,
unless a grain of wheat falls into the earth and
dies,
it remains alone;
but if it dies,
it bears much fruit."

All ego-centeredness must be subordinated, just as Jesus places his ego at the disposal of the Father and the lost of the world, and the Father gives the most costly gift of his Son.

Since this is the way of the Son and the Father, it must also be the way of believers who are to emulate the selfless and self-giving nature of the divine Family (this essential teaching is also found in Matt. 10:39; 16:25; Mark 8:35; Luke 9:24; 14:26):

12:25 "He who loves his life loses it,
and he who hates his life in this world
will keep it for eternal life."

Jesus makes himself the focus of servanthood as representative voice of the divine Society and claims the right to use the authoritative "I am" which brings the faithful servant into fellowship with that Community. When the believer serves the Son he also serves the Father, for the Father honors service done unto the Son as though it were done unto himself. Thus the Father defers to the Son as spokesman for the divine Family:

12:26 "If any one serves me, he must follow me;
and where I am, there shall my servant be also;
if any one serves me, the Father will honor him."

Jesus embodies the generosity and availability that characterize the essential relationships within the divine Community and within the derivative family of believers he is bringing into being. His anguished prayer attests the costliness of the gift of divine hospitality as the hour of final suffering draws near and he rejects the temptation to abort it for selfish reasons; for upon his faithful decision to evince the generosity of the First Family by going to the cross hangs the entire purpose of his coming: to glorify the Father, to lift up a family of believers, and to bring righteous judgment upon an unbelieving and selfish world with its ruler. The temptation to avoid the cross is overcome in obedience to the Father in fulfillment of the redemptive drama. Oneness and faithfulness are crucial at this point, and Jesus, completely selfless in his act of consecration, makes himself wholly transparent to the glory of the Father:

12:27 "Now is my soul troubled. And what shall I say?
'Father, save me from this hour'?
No, for this purpose I have come to this hour.
12:28 Father, glorify thy name."

The unifying aim of the persons of the divine Society is always to be pleasing to one another, and the prayer of Jesus evokes a pleasing response from the Father to whom it is addressed. The Father speaks in accord with the glorifying purpose of the Son, affirming that the Son's ministry to this point and on the cross to come does bring glory. The Father's approval of the work of the Son implies their mutual glorification and reiterates the approval of the Son by the divine Family at the baptism (John 1:32–34; Matt. 3:13–17; Mark 1:9–11; Luke 3:21–22) and at the transfiguration (Matt. 17:1–8; Mark 9:2–8; Luke 9:28–36):

12:28 Then a voice came from heaven,
"I have glorified it,
and I will glorify it again."

The voice of the Father is meant to accompany and approve Jesus' words, but only Jesus clearly understands its meaning. Accordingly he indicts his audience who hear only thunder or misinterpret the Father's voice as being the voice of an angel; for the voice, Jesus says, is meant for them, not for him (12:29–30). He asserts that the judgment of the world has come and its ruler will be cast out (12:31), referring to the hour that has been set in motion and that will culminate at the cross when he will be lifted up. Jesus' use of the personal pronouns *I* and *myself* seems to focus the drama of redemptive history upon himself, but the passive "am lifted up" implies the role of the Father in the event and the unity of the divine Family in working together for the salvation and judgment of the world:

12:32 "And I, when I am lifted up from the earth,
will draw all men to myself."

Although Jesus says, "I will draw all men to myself," the same verb (*helkō*) in an earlier passage also describes the work of the Father in conjunction with the Son, bearing evidence that salvation is a work of the Society of divine persons:

6:44   "No one can come to me
unless the Father who sent me draws him;
and I will raise him up
at the last day."

The evangelist observes that Jesus' figure of being lifted up was "to show by what death he was to die" (12:33). Pitted against this central act of divine disposability which brings eternal life to the lost is the questioning crowd. There is no place in their theology for a disposable Christ, for in their view Christ remains forever without any need to be lifted up; their Messiah is not a suffering Messiah. Nor do they understand who the Son of man is (12:34). Jesus does not answer their unbelief directly but affirms that he is light incarnate. He summons them to believe while there is still time, that they may become sons of light and members of the redeemed society. The First Family is begetting a redeemed family, but it can be entered into only by a voluntary decision to be at the disposal of Jesus who is the light:

12:35   "The light is with you for a little longer.
Walk while you have the light,
lest the darkness overtake you;
he who walks in the darkness does not know
where he goes.
12:36   While you have the light, believe in the light,
that you may become sons of light."

The evangelist describes the unbelieving response of Jesus' audience at large and the halfhearted belief of some of the authorities who "loved the praise of men more than the praise of God" (12:36–43). Against this backdrop of rejection Jesus cries out with an invitation that clearly witnesses to his unity with and deference to the Father, signifying that his person and ministry have no other purpose than to manifest the will of the Father. The concluding passage strongly emphasizes the characteristics of deference, admiration, consecration, and availability that define the inner relationships of the divine Community as it generously pours itself out for a fallen world. Jesus' invitation to believe in himself indicates his sense of equality with the Father, but he immediately shifts the point of reference from himself to the Father, at whose disposal he stands in complete servanthood and faithfulness, taking none of the credit or glory for himself:

12:44 "He who believes in me, believes not in me
but in him who sent me."

He now shifts the focus back to himself as the one who reveals him who has sent him, signifying the unity and equality of Son and Father, for to see the Son is to see the Father. Yet the fact that Jesus says that he is sent has the effect of transferring glory back to the Father. There is a dynamic of reciprocity in the language of the Son:

12:45 "And he who sees me
sees him who sent me."

Once again Jesus occupies the central position as he claims to be the light of the world and the legitimate object of belief, the source of divine generosity to those who walk in darkness:

12:46 "I have come as light into the world,
that whoever believes in me
may not remain in darkness."

Again Jesus claims the divine focus and his implied equality with God, for it is in terms of him and his sayings that a person is saved. That he disclaims the role of judging implies his deference to the Father who does judge, although it is in terms of his suffering and the cross that the world is now being judged (12:31–32). The principal object of his ministry, however, is to save, not to condemn (cf. 3:17–21):

85

12:47 "If any one hears my sayings and does not keep
them,
I do not judge him;
for I did not come to judge the world
but to save the world."

Nevertheless, it is Jesus' words that will condemn the unbeliever on the day of judgment, for the words of Jesus reflect the righteousness of God, since he is the Logos of 1:1
and 1:14 who is with God, is God, and "became flesh and
dwelt among us, full of grace and truth." Hence Jesus can
say:

12:48 "He who rejects me and does not receive my
sayings
has a judge;
the word that I have spoken
will be his judge on the last day."

Having made his self-attestation and cast the final judgment of the world in terms of his spoken word, Jesus again
makes himself subsidiary to the Father and leaves no doubt
that he does not stand alone as an independent "I" but is in
essence one with the Father whose word he has received and
spoken. The alternation between Jesus' authoritative "I" and
"me" (12:45, 46, 48) and the authority of the Father (12:45,
49) continues the paradox of oneness and individuality that
defines the divine Community in the Gospel:

12:49 "For I have not spoken on my own authority;
the Father who sent me has himself given me
commandment
what to say and what to speak."

Jesus' complete disposability to the Father evinces the
solidarity of the divine Family and his disposition to be totally transparent to the one whose commandment is life.
Jesus' characteristic response is to lend himself spontane-
ously in a gift of self as servant to the Father. His attitude is
marked by a sense of "feeling at home" with the mind of the
Father. Interpersonal communion and immersion in the will

of the other would further define Jesus' voluntary assimilation to the thought of the Father, to whom he is joyously hospitable and faithful. Jesus' "I" is wholly identified with the Father's; and because it is, he speaks as the very voice of God. His speech is the Father's speech:

12:50   "And I know that his commandment is eternal
              life.
          What I say, therefore, I say
            as the Father has bidden me."

In this episode Jesus has underscored once more the unity of Father and Son and implied that the reciprocal relationship of the persons of the divine Community ensures that even the most deferential referral of glory to the Father by the Son attests the equality of the Son with the Father. This inference further enrages his adversaries to action against him, for they correctly understand this much of Jesus' language, that he is claiming to speak as the voice of God. Jesus has again made the astounding claim that he is spokesman for the divine Community.

4

The Triune Community of Father, Son, and Holy Spirit
John 13–16

The drama of the fourth Gospel now moves to a more intimate stage as the action of the salvation story is enacted in smaller family circles where discourse takes place between disciples and master (chaps. 13–16) and Son and Father (chap. 17).

The Son and the New Community
Chapter 13

In the opening text of chapter 13, the evangelist describes a high dramatic moment before Jesus' arrest and crucifixion: "Now before the feast of the Passover, when Jesus knew that his hour had come to depart out of this world to the Father, having loved his own who were in the world, he loved them to the end" (13:1). Noteworthy in this introduction to the final act of Jesus' ministry is language that is redolent of the social nature of God and the emerging community of believers. Jesus is the Son (implied) who knows that his departure to the Father is near. He has loved his own, a reference to the redeemed family of believers, and he has loved them with faithful constancy to the end. The faithful availability of the Son to the Father is reflected in hospitable love to his own, in contrast to the infidelity of Judas Iscariot who images in his heart a demonic selfishness and indisposability. This ironic contrast, highlighting the infinite distance between the social and the antisocial, takes place at supper, the consummate image of intimate fellowship and nourishment (cf. chap. 6).

Jesus, the evangelist intimates, "knowing that the Father had given all things into his hands, and that he had come from God and was going to God" (13:3), is conscious of his unity and equality with the Father and of his role as servant. Through his acted and spoken language Jesus uses the occasion of communal eating to teach his disciples something profoundly true of the ultimate Community, whose fellowship, oneness, and mutual disposability he represents. He is about to demonstrate in the humble act of footwashing what divine love is like and what the disciples' relationship to one another should reflect. When Jesus the Son rises from supper, lays aside his garments, pours water into a basin, and begins to wash the disciples' feet, wiping them with the towel with which he is girded (13:4–5), he is the incarnation of the essential nature of the divine Community which is radically hospitable and self-giving. All of Jesus' words and acts to this moment have expressed this fundamental theme of the divine Society whose inexhaustible dynamism is characterized by hospitality. The drama of the Son of the Father, on his knees before his disciples in need of washing from their sin, epitomizes the loving humility of the servant who is there for the other. Jesus exemplifies in his own behavior the characteristic motif of the divine Community and of the beloved community he is bringing into being.

Also present is the theme of participation that is essential to hospitality and accounts for the essential unity of the participants, who nonetheless do not lose their individuality. The two essential elements of the divine Society, unity and individuality, are reflected in the relationship of Jesus to the disciples and they to him. In reply to Peter's objection that Jesus will never wash his feet (13:6–8a), Jesus observes, "If I do not wash you, you have no part in me" (13:8b). By this he indicates that the believing community is constituted through participation in him. The disciples participate in Jesus, as Peter is invited to do, by making themselves available to the generosity of Jesus. One gives, the other receives, in mutual hospitality and disposability that make interpersonal communion and the new community possible. Whoever refuses to be washed by Jesus rejects the way of hospitality which is the only access to the redeemed community, for the washing prophetically anticipates the washing of the cross.

Jesus is inviting his disciples to acknowledge that humility and servanthood are essential characteristics of divine love and must characterize the new society. This fact is borne out in his instructions following the footwashing. He asks them whether they know what he has done to them (13:12), and proceeds to explain its social implications. He does not hesitate to acknowledge that they rightly call him Teacher and Lord, "for so I am," he says (13:13), asserting his right to be the focus of their respect and authority and to stand in the very place of God himself. But because this is true, and as he has at the same time humbled himself and placed himself utterly at their disposal, the implication for them is clear. The analogy is from the top down, from the Son in the divine Community to the disciples in the redeemed community. The availability of the Son to the disciples must be matched by the availability of disciple to disciple:

13:14   "If I, then, your Lord and Teacher,
       have washed your feet,
   you also ought to wash
       one another's feet.
13:15   For I have given you an example,
       that you also should do
       as I have done to you."

Jesus implies that there is no place in God's new society for pride and self-centeredness, for the Son of God is himself a servant. If the Son is first a servant to the Father and then a servant to his disciples, it is imperative that his disciples be servants of the Son and servants of one another. The disciple cannot claim immunity from servanthood in view of the fact that the master himself is a servant in the highest sense:

13:16   "Truly, truly, I say to you,
       a servant is not greater than his master;
       nor is he who is sent greater than he who sent
         him."

91

Jesus himself defers to the Father and does not imagine that he is greater than the Father, although he is conscious of being one with the Father. God the divine Community is dynamically social both inwardly and outwardly in unselfish hospitality. This truth about ultimate reality, Jesus implies, is the secret to true disciplehood and true community. As the Son is faithful and blessed in giving himself away, so his disciples will be blessed if they are faithful in giving themselves away. But knowledge of this truth must be translated into decisive action:

13:17 "If you know these things,
blessed are you if you do them."

Not all choose the way of servanthood. Some follow the dark way of self-interest and self-service at the expense of Jesus and the new community, like Judas who is the antithesis of Jesus, Son and servant. The antisocial betrayal of Jesus by Judas exemplifies the evil of one who knows what is true but does not do it, has participated in Jesus' generosity but has not reciprocated. Judas, together with his associates among the religious authorities and the dark power that lies behind them, is opposed to all that Jesus stands for as incarnate generosity. Mindful of Judas, Jesus claims the validity of prophetic Scripture and the fulfillment of Psalm 41:9 in the sovereign divine plan. The irony is that Judas the rebel has already been graciously sustained by the bread of the Lord's table, yet uses its nourishment and intimacy to betray Jesus, thus unwittingly fulfilling the divine prophecy of betrayal. Jesus declares that human rebellion cannot thwart the sovereignty of God:

13:18 "I am not speaking of you all;
I know whom I have chosen;
it is that the scripture may be fulfilled,
'He who ate my bread
has lifted his heel against me.' "

Jesus' use of the personal pronoun *I* affirms his confidence that he has the authority to predict the imminent betrayal of

Judas so that his disciples may be assured that he is truly the Son of God, the "I am" (*egō eimi*):

13:19   "I tell you this now,
> before it takes place,
> that when it does take place
> > you may believe that I am he."

Jesus concludes this discourse on a positive note of belief and receptivity in view of the emerging new community of faith that he as the Son of God is bringing into being. The secret of God's reality is that each member of the community is a servant who is sent to share. In receiving the divine sharing the new believer receives not only the witness, but also Jesus the Son who sent him, and not only Jesus the Son, but also the Father who sent him. Jesus traces the dynamic of the family mission of servanthood backward to its origin in the divine Family. The generosity of the witnessing family of believers to new believers should lead all to acknowledge the generosity of the Son and the generosity of the Father. The progression of divine love stems from the generous and loving disposability of Father to Son, Son to believer, and believer to believer:

13:20   "Truly, truly, I say to you,
> he who receives any one whom I send
> > receives me;
> and he who receives me
> > receives him who sent me."

After the tense and sorrowful exchange with Judas following supper, and after Judas, having rejected the community of God, departs into the night (13:21–30), Jesus speaks of his glorification against the dark background of this tragic rejection, affirming that unbelief and selfish rebellion cannot destroy the reality of God's family but become ironically and providentially the means to its realization in the cross. The unity and equality of Father and Son are evidenced in their mutual glorification by the suffering of the Son:

13:31 When he had gone out, Jesus said,
          "Now is the Son of man glorified,
          and in him God is glorified."

The mutual glorification of Father and Son is expressed again by Jesus as he repeats the theme of the Father's glorification in the Son and the Son's glorification in the Father. Verses 31 and 32 form a chiasm in which the first and last declarations (*a* and *a'*) describe the glorification of the Son, and the two middle statements (*b* and *b'*) the glorification of the Father. The individuality and unity of Father and Son are both attested in Jesus' parallel declaration:

13:32 "If God is glorified in him,
          God will also glorify him in himself,
          and glorify him at once."

Jesus now looks to the cross and informs the disciples that where he is going they cannot come (13:33, 36–38), for the new community of God is something only the Son in his faithfulness as representative of the divine Community can bring into being, at great cost. What characterizes the divine Society and the new society of believers is the love that originates in the First Family, is manifested in the Son, empowers the community of the faithful, and sets them apart in the world. Believers are to be at one another's disposal in the new community, just as Jesus has been lovingly at their disposal. The characteristic mark of believers as disciples of the Son is to reflect his self-giving love among themselves:

13:34 "A new commandment I give to you,
          that you love one another;
          even as I have loved you,
          that you also love one another.
13:35 By this all men will know
          that you are my disciples,
          if you have love for one another."

Jesus returns to the warning (13:33) that they cannot come where he is going (13:36–38), for the cross requires a

94

sacrifice of the Son who has been in perfect and unbroken fellowship with the Father. The new society cannot come into being until the perfectly faithful and loving Son lays down his life for the lost. Salvation is by grace alone. Even Peter will deny his Lord three times (13:38). Once Jesus has given his life, he intimates that his disciples will follow in his ministry of suffering love for others. After the price has been paid to redeem and empower the new community, they will follow in the mission of telling others about his love, washing the feet of the needy, and suffering on his behalf for one another (cf. Col. 1:24):

13:36 "Where I am going you cannot follow me now;
 but you shall follow afterward."

The Home of the Triune Community
Chapter 14

Chapter 14 should be considered a continuation of the discourse in the previous chapter. The disciples are troubled by Jesus' prediction of his separation and death, and he responds to their need for comfort and assurance by placing himself, in his hour of greatest need, at their disposal, attesting further the selfless hospitality of the divine Community. Peace, truth, and joy are thematic in this chapter and flow out of Jesus' confident sense of "going home" to prepare a dwelling place for his disciples. The role of the Spirit in the ministry of the Triune Community is explicitly mentioned in Jesus' discourse and is seen to be in accord with the theme of availability and hospitality that has been characteristic of Father and Son in the Gospel to this point. Family images are striking, from the very beginning of the comforting discourse. Jesus reiterates his equality with the Father by inviting belief in himself as well as in God as an antidote to the troubled heart:

14:1 "Let not your hearts be troubled;
 believe in God,
 believe also in me."

95

The Father's house (*oikia*) of many rooms (*monai pollai*) is the central image in the ecology (literally, "a study of the house") of the new community the Triune Society is calling into being. Jesus' nature is to speak the absolute truth; he describes the reality of a dwelling place for the new family of God, and the fact that at the cost of great suffering he is going to prepare a place for them in the Father's house. Jesus the Son together with the Father is opening their home in supreme hospitality to those who believe the promise is true:

14:2   "In my Father's house are many rooms;
if it were not so, would I have told you
that I go to prepare a place for you?"

Jesus speaks as the voice of the divine Community and generously promises to make his dwelling place the dwelling place of believers. His authoritative "I go," "I will come," and "I am" are the credentials that assure the disciples that he is telling the truth and is offering them a genuine homecoming which his going and his coming again will bring to reality:

14:3   "And when I go and prepare a place for you,
I will come again and will take you to myself,
that where I am you may be also."

Thomas, voicing the disciples' perplexity about Jesus' destination and their wonderment as to the way (14:5), invites Jesus' response that he is not only the way but also the only way to the Father. Jesus' consciousness of equality with the Father is dramatically stated as he claims to be not only the way of salvation but also the center of truth and life, which are attributes of God. Jesus implies that all pluralistic theologies that teach many ways to God are false, for the only way to the Father's house and to participation in the Family of God is through him. Ultimate reality is social, but access to this realm is only through the Son who gives his life with divine charity that those who are unworthy of life might come home. There can be no homecoming except in terms of the Host, who requires that the invited guests be redeemed and washed before entering. Redemption and washing adequate to the homecoming come only through the generosity of the suffering Son, who represents the generosity of the divine Society. Because of his redemptive suffering, the Son is the way, the truth, and the life. Belief in Jesus and his redeeming work is absolutely necessary for entry into God's household and community. Thus Jesus can speak authoritatively as the "I am":

14:6 "I am the way, and the truth, and the life;
no one comes to the Father,
but by me."

Jesus continues his discourse to his disciples with the parallel thought that to know the Son is to know the Father, and he promises that they will know the Father; indeed, they have already seen him incarnate in himself. In his decisive equation of himself and the Father he implies not only that the Father has deferred to him in manifesting himself in the Son, but also that to know one is to know the other. Jesus makes a strong statement about his incarnate self, for he claims that God is truly incarnate in him. He promises that his disciples will come to know him, implying the cross and the gift of the Holy Spirit, and have in fact already seen the Father embodied in the Son. The divine Community is already present in the generous reality and promise of Jesus the incarnate Son:

14:7 "If you had known me,
you would have known my Father also;
henceforth you know him
and have seen him."

Philip's request that Jesus show the disciples the Father fails to grasp the truth of Jesus' disclosure, even though Jesus has been manifesting the Father to his disciples for so long a time (14:8). Jesus remonstrates with Philip and implies that the disciple needs to place himself at the Son's disposal and believe; when he does he will see that the Son and the Father are one, and that the incarnate Jesus reveals the divine Society, for the Father discloses himself in the Son:

14:9   "Have I been with you so long,
            and yet you do not know me, Philip?
        He who has seen me has seen the Father;
            how can you say, 'Show us the Father'?"

Jesus then asks a rhetorical question which amounts to a declaration that the Son and the Father mutually indwell one another, so that while they are distinct persons, they are nevertheless one. The faithful disciple must believe in the equality and mutuality of the Son and the Father in the divine Community:

14:10a "Do you not believe that I am in the Father
            and the Father in me?"

After speaking for an extended period of his coequality with the Father Jesus defers to the Father as the source of his authority, then further defines the mutual indwelling in terms of mutual deference: Father and Son, although two persons, indwell one another so that the Son can say that what he does the Father does. The Son makes himself available to the Father, and the Father defers to work through the Son:

14:10b "The words that I say to you
            I do not speak on my own authority;
        but the Father who dwells in me
            does his works."

It is necessary for the disciples to believe that Jesus is in the Father and that the Father is in Jesus, for they are one; but if they cannot bring themselves to believe that fact, then a lesser necessary belief is that they recognize that the works Jesus is doing are evidence of the Father working in him, for Jesus' works do indeed manifest the presence of the divine Community in human redemption:

98

14:11 "Believe me that I am in the Father
and the Father in me;
or else believe me
for the sake of the works themselves."

As the Father is in the Son, so in an analogous way, Jesus says, believers in him will be enabled to do the works that he does, even greater works, as a consequence of his going to the Father. Jesus is referring to the completion of his suffering servanthood on earth and the giving of the enabling power of the Spirit, by which the disciples will carry on the work of the redeemed community. Jesus speaks with the authoritative "Truly, truly, I say" formula, promising that the disciple who places himself at the disposal of the Son will bring even more lost members home to the family, because Jesus will make it possible by his return to the Father. The theme of the extended, dynamic community is implicit in Jesus' prophetic declaration:

14:12 "Truly, truly, I say to you, he who believes in me
will also do the works that I do;
and greater works than these will he do,
because I go to the Father."

Mutual disposability describes the new community, as Jesus offers to be wholly available to the requests of his followers who have placed themselves at his service, all to the glory of the Father. Hospitality identifies the divine Society and the new society:

14:13 "Whatever you ask in my name,
I will do it,
that the Father may be glorified
in the Son;
14:14 if you ask anything in my name,
I will do it."

Jesus has spoken of empowering the disciples by going to the Father (14:12), and he now expounds what that promise implies. First, there is the expectation that they will love the Son by keeping his commandments, and his commandments are summed up in the one great commandment of 13:34: "A new commandment I give to you, that you love one another; even as I have loved you, that you also love one another." Thus Jesus can call them to account in terms of his own charitable example, for his commandments are not abstractions but are what define the divine Triunity. Jesus is the person who represents that Community of love. His appeal to his disciples therefore is that they emulate him as person rather than adhere to abstract principles, for love has no reality of its own apart from its embodiment in the persons of the divine Community, whom Jesus represents. Accordingly, he declares that if they love him they will indeed be keeping his commandments. He does not say that if they love him the commandments are something they will feel compelled to keep in addition to that love (note the interchangeability of "love" and "commandments" in v. 21):

14:15   "If you love me,
    you will keep my commandments."

Jesus now refers to the third member of the Triune Family who will be given as a gift to the disciples as a result of Jesus' going to the Father. The divine Community is fully at the disposal of the new society as Jesus charitably prays the Father, who in turn generously gives the Paraclete, who places himself hospitably at the disposal of the disciples. The interpersonal communion of the Triune Society is essentially an interaction of being there for the other: the Father listens to the request of the Son, and the Paraclete listens to the request of the Father and of the Son. All three persons of the Triune Community are at one another's disposal and place themselves at the disposal of the new community. Jesus describes both the Paraclete and himself as counselors or advocates of the disciples. They will always have an advocate, for the Paraclete will be with them forever:

14:16   "And I will pray the Father,
    and he will give you another Counselor,
    to be with you for ever,

14:17   even the Spirit of truth,
>   whom the world cannot receive,
>   because it neither sees him nor knows him;
>   you know him,
>   for he dwells with you, and will be in you."

There are three constituencies here: (1) the Spirit of truth, representative of the Triune Society, who is forever available (2) to believers; and (3) the world which rejects the generosity of the Triune Family because it lives in untruth and therefore can never see the Spirit or know him. Not all the world, therefore, responds to God's love or participates in the new community.

Jesus assures the disciples of his faithful presence with them, a theme with which the discourse begins in 14:1–3. The primary image is of being at home and of being together in family fellowship and love, where hospitality and interpersonal communion abound. The following promises are therefore assurances of the Triune Family, although they are couched in the representative "I" of the Son. Anticipating his death and resurrection, Jesus prophesies his physical departure from the world and his spiritual return to those who have eyes of faith. Jesus restates his promise that he will be available to them and will share his life with them, implying that as the Lord of life he is fashioning a community of life. The family image of interpersonal communion and love is heightened by a literal translation of *orphanous* in verse 18a ("I will not leave you orphans"), which, expressed positively, means that Jesus the Son in the divine Family is promising his disciples adoption as children in the Family circle:

14:18   "I will not leave you desolate (*orphanous*);
>   I will come to you.
14:19   Yet a little while,
>   and the world will see me no more,
>   but you will see me;
>   because I live,
>   you will live also."

101

Consciously fulfilling the numerous Old Testament prophecies that anticipate an eschatological day of renewal ("In that day," e.g., Isa. 11:10–11; 26:1–4), Jesus the Son speaks in intimate Family images of the Son indwelling the Father, believers the Son, and the Son his followers. The divine Reality is social to the core:

> **14:20** "In that day you will know
> that I am in my Father,
> and you in me,
> and I in you."

If the believer possesses the love commandments of Jesus and places himself at his disposal, he manifests his love for the Son in his behavior and is loved by the Son's Father because of their coequality in the divine Family. The hospitable love of Father and Son is evident as the believer is drawn into the orbit of the Family and mirrors its essential characteristics of belonging, accessibility, and charity:

> **14:21** "He who has my commandments and keeps
> them,
> he it is who loves me;
> and he who loves me
> will be loved by my Father,
> and I will love him
> and manifest myself to him."

Responding to the question of Judas (not Iscariot) why he will not manifest himself to all (14:22), Jesus implies that membership in the divine Society requires loving the Son and obediently doing his will. A rebellious spirit that does not love the Son or do his will has no place in the community. The theme of interpersonal communion (14:21) is repeated as Jesus explicitly identifies this mutual indwelling as the hospitable gift of the divine Family who come to make their home (*monēn*) with the believer:

> **14:23** "If a man loves me,
> he will keep my word,
> and my Father will love him,

> and we will come to him
> and make our home with him."

The unbeliever can be known by the company he keeps (cf. Matt. 7:16–20: "You will know them by their fruits"). Not all will be saved and enter into fellowship with the Family of God, but only those who make themselves accessible to the Son by keeping his words, just as the Son makes himself accessible to the Father by keeping his word. The Family circle is defined in terms of fidelity to what is spoken by Father and Son:

14:24 "He who does not love me
does not keep my words;
and the word which you hear is not mine
but the Father's who sent me."

Jesus' use of the possessive pronoun *my* ("my word," v. 23, "my words," v. 24) expresses his conscious individuality as the person who is Son in the divine Family. His disclaimer in verse 24b ("not mine but the Father's who sent me") does not nullify or contradict his own personal possession of the authoritative word, but signals his unity with the Father. Thus the two aspects of oneness and individuality within the divine Community are seen to be inseparable: "me," "my," "Father"/"we" (v. 23).

Jesus' image of home (*monē*) in 14:23 is expressed in terms of the Triune Family in verses 25–26 and parallels the image at the beginning of the discourse (vv. 1–3) and the divine Triunity in verses 16–17. The Holy Spirit/Paraclete is sent by the Father and the Son to carry on the work of indwelling the believing fellowship and to bring to remembrance all that Jesus the Son has said to them, and what the Father has said to the Son. Father, Son, and Holy Spirit are one in what they speak because their persons are united in dynamic participation and availability that spill over in hospitality to the new society of believers. Jesus the Son is the incarnate Speaker, the Logos of 1:1, 14, who gives grace upon grace from his fullness during the days of his flesh (1:16–18):

14:25 "These things I have spoken to you,
while I am still with you."

But once the work of the incarnate Son is completed, the Holy Spirit is sent by the Father in the name of the Son to bring to remembrance what the Son has said and done. The presence of the Holy Spirit in the work of remembrance not only attests the historical authenticity of John's Gospel, but also further discloses the intimate interrelationship of Father, Son, and Holy Spirit and their mutual deference to one another. The Father defers to the Holy Spirit by sending him in his place, and defers to the Son by sending the Holy Spirit in Jesus' name. Son and Holy Spirit defer to the Father by going obediently and generously on behalf of the Father; and all three persons of the Triune Family defer hospitably to the new family of believers. The Triune God is at their disposal to draw them into the covenanted language of the Family circle by calling to remembrance the spoken and acted words of Jesus the Son:

14:26 "But the Counselor, the Holy Spirit,
whom the Father will send in my name,
he will teach you all things,
and bring to your remembrance
all that I have said to you."

Jesus promises that the Holy Spirit will teach the disciples the Triune Family's interpretation of historical events by preserving in inspired memory what its spokesman the Son has said and done in space and time. Jesus implies that the disciples are not now in a position to interpret correctly the significance of what they are seeing and hearing, but they will be taught all things by the Holy Spirit and will be given the gift of remembrance. He implies that only within the divine Family's own interpretation of his words and acts can the facts be known as they really are. Jesus is here laying the hermeneutical foundation for a credible exegesis of the gospel material.

Jesus now closes this word to his disciples by reiterating the assurances given earlier, promising them peace and exhorting them not to be troubled in heart (14:27), for the prospect of his leaving them, while fraught with suffering and grief for a time, makes possible the Son's return to the Father to prepare the divine home for them, and his coming again (14:1–3). Jesus' "I" is virtually interchangeable with the person of the Holy Spirit, for it is the Paraclete who is to come at Jesus' departure (14:26; 16–17). This evidences the unity of the divine Community, for it is also implied that the Father as well as the Son will be at home in the believer (14:23). To speak of the presence and the coming of one is to include the other two, for the Triune Family is inseparable:

14:28a "You heard me say to you,
'I go away,
and I will come to you.' "

Jesus the obedient and deferential Son acclaims the Father as greater than he in language that is typical of the divine disposability, where none of the persons exults over the other, but each defers to the other with loving hospitality and availability. The subordination theme also refers to Jesus' incarnate existence as servant. If the disciples really loved Jesus the Son (as they will come to love him and know him through the Holy Spirit), they would understand that his imminent departure to the Father means that his future glorification is greater than his present and humble incarnate life in the flesh; hence, "the Father is greater than I" reflects the deference of incarnate Son to Father. Yet in light of other paradoxical utterances, it would seem that here again the Son is making a statement that tells us something of his attitude toward the Father within the divine Triunity itself: the Son subordinates himself to the Father not because he is less than the Father but because it is the nature of all three persons of the Triune Family to subordinate themselves to one another in ultimate deferential love and hospitality. Jesus also expects deferential love and hospitality from his disciples. It is simply and profoundly the way Jesus the Son thinks and speaks that he says to them:

14:28b   "If you loved me, you would have rejoiced,
          because I go to the Father;
       for the Father is greater than I."

Similarly at the close of the discourse, as Jesus predicts the coming of the ruler of this world who will curtail his speaking in the final suffering of the cross (although he has no ultimate power over the Son), Jesus places himself again at the disposal of the Father in obedient love, that the world may know of his love for the Father:

14:31   "But I do as the Father has commanded me,
          so that the world may know
             that I love the Father."

The Vine and Branches, and the Spirit
Who Proceeds from Father and Son
Chapter 15

The discourse at supper concludes as Jesus calls upon his disciples to "rise, [and] go hence" (14:31c). Since Jesus continues with a new discourse in 15:1, it is possible to imagine that he makes his way with the disciples to the next stage of the final hour, perhaps to Gethsemane, and continues to instruct them on the journey. If that is so, Jesus' reference to the vine and the branches might very well be drawn from the pastoral setting along the way, which affords an apt analogy by which to instruct the disciples further about the new community the divine Community is calling into being. Jesus focuses the attention of his followers on himself as the vine, claiming that he is the reality of which the natural vine, and Israel the vine, are only images (e.g., Ps. 80:8–19; Isa. 5:1–7; Ezek. 15; 19:10–14). Jesus is claiming in effect to be the original whom all other vines in the fallen order of nature poorly imitate. He uses the personal pronoun *I* in his typically authoritative manner, disclosing his consciousness of being the center of life. Abiding in him brings life and fruitfulness to the believer; not abiding in him means death and destruction for the unbeliever. In portraying himself as the original vine, Jesus describes an intimate relationship between himself and the Father; one has a sense of the divine Community working together to bring the faithful branches into vital and healthy relationship to the vine, as they are pruned to produce more fruit. There is also judgment of all that is not vitally one with the vine and does not bear fruit. In using the metaphor of the vine and its branches, Jesus implies that the order of creation illustrates the social nature of reality and bears the signature of the social God who has made it. As spokesman for the divine Society, Jesus describes who he is: "I am the true vine" (*Egō eimi hē ampelos hē alēthinē*). He is the original, the archetype, the true vine, set off from all false vines. The Father serves the vine as the vinedresser (*ho geōrgos*) and is at the disposal of the Son:

15:1 "I am the true vine,
and my Father is the vinedresser."

The Father as vinedresser serves the Son by taking away every branch that bears no fruit, while Father and Son, vinedresser and vine, are both at the disposal of the fruitful branches to make them more fruitful. The metaphor is a social image: those who are destructive of the community are removed; those who bear fruit are pruned to bear more fruit. The divine Community is generously disposed to promote the health and productivity of the believing community:

15:2 "Every branch of mine that bears no fruit,
he takes away,
and every branch that does bear fruit
he prunes,
that it may bear more fruit."

Jesus' use of the personal pronouns *I* and *me* in 15:3–7 evidences his claims to correlativity with God the Father, for the mutual abiding of the natural vine and its branches illustrates the interpersonal abiding of Son and Father, and of Jesus and his disciples; the social God who is the source of life abides in the community of believers and they in him. The image implies that as Father, Son, and Spirit mutually abide in one another, so in an analogous way the divine

107

Society and the new society abide in one another. The persons of the divine Family are concerned that the family of believers bear fruit by reflecting divine generosity, and this comes from abiding in the Son. To abide or remain (*menein*) in the Son is prerequisite to bearing much fruit (*pherein karpon polun*); apart from the mutual abiding of branch in vine and vine in branch, one can do nothing that is ultimately of any value, but is cast forth, withers, and is burned (15:5–6).

To abide in the Son who is the vine, however, leads to inexhaustible productivity, for Jesus promises that where there is mutual abiding the disciple may ask whatever he will, and it shall be done for him (15:7), for the Son is at the disposal of the disciples in the name of the Father. When the abiding community makes itself available to the Son in prayerful request, it bears much fruit; thus both Father and Son are glorified as the believing community images the original fruitbearing of the divine Community and becomes a new family of God that is characterized by availability and generosity. Although Jesus does not specifically define fruitbearing in his discourse, very likely it ought to be understood in view of his own ministry of suffering and disposability: "Truly, truly, I say to you, unless a grain of wheat falls into the earth and dies, it remains alone; but if it dies, it bears much fruit" (12:24). Bearing fruit is therefore an attitude of being there for the other, as the disciple gives himself in service to the glory of God, and in faithful witness to others who are yet to come into the community. The Father is glorified and the Son is honored by living proof when the new society acts like Father and Son:

15:8   "By this my Father is glorified,
        that you bear much fruit,
        and so prove to be my disciples."

The loving generosity of Father to Son is the original from which flows the redemptive love of Son to believers. As the Father makes himself available to the Son, so the Son makes himself available to believers. The direction of love is first from the top down, from the divine Society to the created order. Once the divine love touches the community of disciples, they are to reciprocate from the bottom upward:

15:9 "As the Father has loved me,
so have I loved you;
abide in my love."

As the Father has loved the Son and the Son has loved the disciples, the appeal of the Son that they abide in his love brings about a completion of the circle as the vector of love now moves from below to its source above. The movement of 15:9 is reversed in 15:10; the believing family of faith is called upon to respond in loving obedience to the Son as the Son responds in loving obedience to the Father. The two sayings exemplify the mutual flow of selfless deference and generosity in both directions between the divine Community and the new society:

15:10 "If you keep my commandments,
you will abide in my love,
just as I have kept my Father's commandments
and abide in his love."

The result of mutual indwelling is a quality that defines the life of the divine Family and the redeemed family of believers: joy (*chara*). Fullness of joy is a social relationship that exists between the persons of the First Family and, by grace, between the Triune Family and the family of disciples. The motivating desire of the Son, who speaks in behalf of the First Community, is to share the divine life with generosity and joy:

15:11 "These things I have spoken to you,
that my joy may be in you,
and that your joy may be full."

The joyful relationship that exists between the persons of the First Family, and between the First Family and the redeemed family of believers, Jesus describes in terms of friendship rather than servanthood (15:12–15). Servants are not able to share as friends do, as indeed the persons of the

109

divine Society share, because servants are not taken into the confidence of the family or apprised of what the master is doing. Generous love and sharing characterize true friendship. The Father shares everything with the Son, and the Son shares all with believers, who, chosen on the initiative of the Son on behalf of the divine Family, are accounted as friends. Jesus the Son speaks as the Logos or Expression of the divine Family and reemphasizes to the disciples their need to love one another as he has loved them. Love is social and is the prelude to friendship:

15:12 "This is my commandment,
that you love one another
as I have loved you."

True friendship is ultimately defined by disposability, the willingness to give everything, including one's life, for the sake of the friend. Jesus has already intimated his willingness to die for his followers (10:11, 15; 12:7, 24), and now again anticipates the cross, where divine disposability intersects with the needs of his fragmented friends, the disciples, to bring them into the circle of the new society:

15:13 "Greater love has no man than this,
that a man lay down his life for his friends."

Friendship in the Family circle is conditional upon the willingness of the disciples to place themselves at the disposal of the Son. There must be a voluntary reciprocity for the circle of friendship to be complete; believers must be one with the will of the Son who speaks with the authoritative "I" of the divine Community of friendship:

15:14 "You are my friends
if you do what I command you."

Jesus the Son continues to speak with the spokesman's authoritative "I" when he calls the faithful knowledgeable friends (*philous*) rather than unknowledgeable servants (*doulous*). The social implications of this declaration are consid-

110

erable, for Jesus shares with his followers his own privileged access to the Father, making known to them what he has heard from his Father. Jesus also implies that just as his privileged access to divine friendship is made possible by his availability as listening servant of the Father, so the privileged access of the disciples to the friendship of the divine Community is realized by their becoming servants of the Son. The paradox is that the privilege of being called friends is a result of first being servants. Once the servant has made himself disposable to the Son, he is taken into the confidence of the Family and is accounted a friend, just as Jesus' love and friendship in the divine Family is inseparable from his faithful accessibility as servant of the Father:

15:15 "No longer do I call you servants,
  for the servant does not know
    what his master is doing;
but I have called you friends,
  for all that I have heard from my Father
    I have made known to you."

Continuing the theme of abiding in and bearing fruit (15:1–10), Jesus declares the sovereign grace and generosity of the divine Community that calls the new community into being and holds it responsible for fruitbearing and love. Jesus claims the sovereign prerogative of appointing the family of believers to particular tasks of bearing fruit that will abide, and of loving one another. Bearing fruit is not only the glorifying of God, but also the mission of bringing others into the new society (4:36; 12:24); the disciples are to "go" and bear fruit confidently, for the generosity of the Father in the name of the Son lies available to them in prayer. Answered prayer is set in the context of the mission of the new society to the lost (cf. 16:23–24). Jesus the Son, the voice of the divine Community, commands that the love that identifies the relationship of the Community also mark the community of believers:

15:16 "You did not choose me,
  but I chose you and appointed you
    that you should go and bear fruit

> and that your fruit should abide;
> so that whatever you ask the Father in my name,
> he may give it to you.

15:17 This I command you,
to love one another."

The joy of love within the divine Family and the redeemed family Jesus now contrasts with the hatred of the world that he and his disciples are experiencing (15:18–16:11). Participation in the divine Family means not only enjoying the creative love and fidelity of an eternal relationship but also, for the period of redemptive activity in the world, experiencing the pain of opposition, hatred, and rejection. Believers in the new community image the love of the persons of the divine Community and also the servanthood of the Son in his suffering ministry to a hostile world. If the disciples are his friends, they are also his servants, and the servant is not greater than his master. The generosity of the divine Family is about to be exhibited in the ultimate act of disposability, the Son's sacrificial death upon the cross. Because the new society is not of the world, the world's animosity is turned against it as against the Son. So unified are Father and Son that hatred of the one is hatred of the other (as hatred of the disciples is hatred of the Son; cf. Acts 9:4–5). Jesus instructs his followers that one of the facts of life in him is antagonism from the outside. While the proclamation of grace is received by the faithful and creates the new society, it is rejected by the hostile who oppose the love of Son and Father and comprise the worldly society. All decisions are social decisions and have social implications, for good or for bad:

15:23 "He who hates me
hates my Father also."

Jesus informs his disciples that his coming has enraged the worldly society by exposing its sinfulness. His words and works have also exposed him, along with the Father, to hostility. The good news he proclaims to the believing becomes a proclamation of wrath to the unbelieving (cf. the dual nature of the *kērygma* in Rom. 1:16–18):

15:24 "If I had not done among them
the works which no one else did,
they would not have sin;
but now they have seen and hated
both me and my Father."

Jesus sees his rejection foretold in Old Testament prophecy (Ps. 35:19; 69:4); thus even the pain of opposition has a deeper meaning in the plan of salvation. In view of the context (15:23–24) where the Father is hated along with the Son, Jesus implies that the Father is also hated without a cause. Worldly hatred of Father and Son is without a cause because the divine Community is the source of community; warfare against it is groundless and self-destructive. There is a subtle irony in the meaning of the expression *without a cause* (LXX, *dōrean*) and the related word *gift* (*dōrea*) which would not escape the evangelist's or the reader's eye:

15:25 "It is to fulfil the word
that is written in their law,
'They hated me without a cause.' "

The Trinity passages in chapter 14 (vv. 15–17, 23, 25–26) are paralleled in the witness saying of 15:26, as Jesus assures the disciples that Father, Son, and Holy Spirit/Paraclete will be with them and witness to them in their witnessing. The Holy Spirit (the Paraclete and Spirit of truth) is at the disposal of Father and Son in the redemptive mission and carries on the work of bearing witness to Jesus the Son, who is bearing witness to the Father. All three persons of the Triune Community are deferring to one another: the Holy Spirit to the Son, the Son to the Father, the Father to the Son's request, and Father and Son to the Spirit in honoring him as witness and truth bearer, making the circle of divine accessibility and hospitality complete. Jesus' promise that the divine Triunity is graciously at the disposal of the believing community describes both the inner relationships that denote the essential love and deference of the persons of the

Trinity to one another, and the external relationship of the Triune Community to the disciples:

15:26 "But when the Counselor comes,
      whom I shall send to you from the Father,
        even the Spirit of truth,
        who proceeds from the Father,
he will bear witness to me."

As Father and Spirit bear witness to the Son, so the disciples are witnesses to the redemptive love of the Triune Family because from the beginning of Jesus' ministry they have comprised the nucleus of the new community. The Triune Community and the new community are dynamically social. Bearing much fruit (15:5) is evidenced in bearing witness:

15:27 "And you also are witnesses,
      because you have been with me
        from the beginning."

The Spirit of Truth, Servant of the Community
Chapter 16

Jesus' earlier comforting discourse, together with his words about the coming suffering of the disciples and the fact that "indeed, the hour is coming when whoever kills you will think he is offering service to God" (16:2), are designed to keep them from falling away (16:1). Hatred and opposition stem from rejection of the claims and generosity of the Triune Family. Jesus speaks of himself and the Father in terms of coequality and traces hostility to a lack of truly knowing him and the Father:

16:3 "And they will do this
      because they have not known the Father,
      nor me."

Jesus returns to the theme of going to the Father who sent him (16:5), and impresses upon his disciples the truth that it is to their advantage that he go away in order that the third person of the Triune Community, the Counselor and Spirit of truth, may come and minister to them and bring the world to account. The language of generosity and hospitality is prominent in Jesus' promise, for the Son completes the work of the Father and returns to him in order that the Paraclete may come. The Triune Family is intimately and equally given to the salvation, preservation, and empowering of the believing family:

16:7   "Nevertheless I tell you the truth:
        it is to your advantage that I go away,
        for if I do not go away,
          the Counselor will not come to you;
        but if I go,
          I will send him to you."

When the Paraclete comes, Jesus assures them, he will witness to the world of the work of the Triune Family in righteousness and judgment. The Spirit of truth comes into the world not only to indwell believers and to bring to remembrance and bear witness (14:15–17, 26; 15:26), but also to convince the unbelieving world of its sin. The Spirit of truth is at the service of the divine Family in carrying out this negative task of judgment. A world that rejects the truth and generosity of the social God will be exposed for its untruth and antisocial rebellion:

16:8   "And when he comes, he will convince the world
        of sin and of righteousness and of judgment:"

Jesus explains the cause of each of the charges against the world. The sin of rejecting Jesus is to be brought to light by the Paraclete:

16:9   "of sin,
        because they do not believe in me;"

The righteous work of the Father, completed on the cross by the righteous Son who returns to the Father in glory, makes possible the righteous judgment by which the Spirit convicts the world:

115

16:10 "of righteousness,
because I go to the Father,
and you will see me no more;"

The Paraclete will demonstrate that the anti-Family ruler of this world is judged by the triumphant work of the Son who ministers on behalf of the Triune Society:

16:11 "of judgment,
because the ruler of this world is judged."

Having described the negative role of the Holy Spirit as judge of the antisocial sin of the world, Jesus turns again to the positive role of the Spirit as generous interpreter of the Triune Family. While Jesus speaks with his authoritative "I" as the Family's spokesman, he defers to the Spirit's authority out of respect for the disciples' weakness and prophesies that the Spirit will speak the words of Father and Son at the proper time, when the Son's work is completed. The Spirit's authority to guide the new community into all truth is the guarantee of the Triune Community that the disciples will be inspired to witness to the truth. Like the Son, the Spirit will not speak independently but will speak what he hears from the Father. No egocentricity or individualism intrudes itself into the Triune Society; the three persons are one God and speak the same message in mutual deference and trust:

16:12 "I have yet many things to say to you,
but you cannot bear them now.
16:13 When the Spirit of truth comes,
he will guide you into all the truth;
for he will not speak on his own authority,
but whatever he hears he will speak,
and he will declare to you
the things that are to come."

In view of the fact that the Holy Spirit is, like Jesus, described as not speaking on his own authority but as proclaiming only what he hears, it is not exegetically feasible to interpret Jesus' listening to the Father (e.g., 8:26, 40) as an insight into his psychological religious development. The listening or "acoustic" (*akouō*) deference of the Spirit to the words of the Son no more means his psychological subordination to the Son than does the listening deference of the Son to the Father imply his religious development. In both cases the expression is an idiom that connotes the voluntary disposability of Son and Spirit as servants of the Triune Community. For them to speak only what they hear signifies the absolute unity of the message of the Triunity. The Father also hears and places himself at the disposal of the Son (11:41–42; 14:16). The persons of the Triune Community are there for one another, to please one another, to hear one another. That is one of the aspects of the consummate love that is exemplified by the social Triunity. Their message is identical because they are essentially one; thus to hear is to be in essential agreement.

That this is the case is clear from 16:14–15. Jesus no longer casts himself in the role of the hearer but assumes the authority of the Father as speaker, for all that the Father has is his. It is now the Spirit of truth who will take what is the Son's and declare it to the disciples. The interchangeability of authority, truth-speaking, and glorification is evident in this trinitarian passage. Jesus implies his equality with the Father when he says that the Spirit will glorify the Son by taking what is his and declaring it to the disciples. The Spirit defers in serving the Son as he serves the community of believers. The Father is for the moment in the background. Jesus then explicitly claims correlativity with the Father, repeating the theme that the Holy Spirit takes what is the Son's and declares it to the disciples. It is the nature of the Triune Community that Father, Son, and Holy Spirit share equally together. What needs to be noted is the angle of vision: at one moment the loving service of all the persons of the Community is highlighted; then the authority and glorification of one of the members, as with Jesus the Son in this passage. The subtle shifts of the listening paradigm clarify the intercommunal nature of the Triunity. The Son claims identity with the Father, complementing his witness as servant of the Father elsewhere. In this unit (16:12–15) Jesus speaks in the place of the Father, and the Spirit plays

117

the role of serving and glorifying the Son, as open hospitality and mutual gifts of self continue to characterize the triune relationship. Each person is fully God and speaks with complete authority, yet each is servant to and witness of the other:

16:14 "He will glorify me,
for he will take what is mine
and declare it to you.
16:15 All that the Father has is mine;
therefore I said that he will take what is mine
and declare it to you."

As the Spirit can speak only the truth, and as the truth characterizes the essential nature of Father, Son, and Holy Spirit, the oneness of the Triune Family is evident in the redemption of the new community. The costly communal process of the disciples' redemption, their coming suffering as well as joy, are spoken of again by Jesus (16:16–24) as he refers to his death and resurrection ("A little while, and you will see me no more; again a little while, and you will see me" [16:16]), and his return to the Father (16:17). Earlier Jesus had spoken of his departure in the discourse about the "Father's house" (14:1–24); he now gives further assurance to the disciples that the sorrowful birth pangs of the cross will turn into joy (16:20–22). At that time all will be made clear, and there will be no need for them to ask questions, for the Father will give them, in the Son's name, anything they ask of him, if they faithfully place themselves at his disposal. The Father places himself completely at the disposal of the believing community, as does Jesus the Son, since the prayer of the disciples flows through the Son to the Father, and back again in response. The divine Family is generously available to the family of believers. Jesus again claims equality with the Father in referring to his own name, making himself and the Family "at home" with the disciples that they may have fullness of joy. Spontaneous, hospitable joy (*chara*) is typically the way of the divine Community:

16:23 "In that day
you will ask nothing of me.
Truly, truly, I say to you,
if you ask anything of the Father,
he will give it to you in my name.
16:24 Hitherto you have asked nothing in my name;
ask, and you will receive,
that your joy may be full."

The language of Jesus has to this point been couched in figures (*en paroimiais*, 16:25, cf. 10:6; *en parabolais*, Mark 4:11). But the hour is coming, Jesus promises, when he will speak plainly (*parrēsia*) of the Father and will no longer need to make special intercession for them (16:25–26). The love of the Father is disclosed through Jesus the Son. When the disciples love the Son and believe that he is from the Father, they love the Father, who loves them. Jesus paints a portrait of a Family of love, unity, and responsive hospitality:

16:27 "For the Father himself loves you,
because you have loved me
and have believed
that I came from the Father."

In a chiasm (*a b b' a'*) that traces the descent of the Son from the Father into the world (in deference to the Father and as servant of the world), to his return from the world to the Father (his work being completed), Jesus portrays the divine fact that the way up is the way down in the U of descent and ascent (cf. Phil. 2:5–11). From the privileged status of the divine Family, to the world of suffering and need, and back to the divine Family, the redemptive activity of Jesus the Son on behalf of the world embodies the dynamic and inexhaustible activity of the persons of the Triune Family who lend themselves to one another within their own Triunity, as Jesus' previous discourses have implied. The ascent to exaltation and glorification is preceded by the gift of self in hospitable servanthood:

16:28 "I came from the Father
and have come into the world;

119

again, I am leaving the world
and going to the Father."

The conclusion of Jesus' confident and consoling words to his disciples (16:29–33) is filled with irony as they claim now to understand, but do not, and are warned that before they learn to be faithful servants they will be scattered and will leave him alone. In that hour, even though the nucleus of the new society is atomized by lack of faith, the social reality of the divine Community coheres, giving hope for the world. In this antithetic contrast, Jesus poignantly describes the lack of family unity among the disciples who will desert him in his final hour; yet the presence of the divine Family ensures that he is not alone, for the Father defers to be with his Son:

16:32 "The hour is coming, indeed it has come,
    when you will be scattered,
    every man to his own home,
      and will leave me alone;
    yet I am not alone,
      for the Father is with me."

In view of this unparalleled act of generosity on the part of the divine Community for the scattered of the world, Jesus concludes his address with consoling words of hope. Because he personally speaks for the Father and the Holy Spirit, Jesus the Son confidently speaks in terms of his authoritative "I" and utters the ultimate word of consolation, offering the nascent community of disciples "the lift of the heart toward home":

16:33 "I have said this to you,
    that in me you may have peace.
    In the world you have tribulation;
      but be of good cheer,
        I have overcome the world."

5

"That They May Be One Even as We Are One"
John 17–21

In Jesus' disclosure of the divine Family the theme that runs repeatedly through his discourses is the generosity of the social God. The manner of Jesus' speech indicates his conviction that the persons of the divine Community inwardly enjoy one another's love, hospitality, generosity, and interpersonal communion, so much so that they are one God, and being one God, express such love to one another. Jesus does not explain the mystery of threeness in oneness and oneness in threeness, but simply allows the fact of God's social nature to emerge in his proclamation that the divine Community extends its hospitality to an inhospitable and fragmented world.

According to the evangelist's prologue, the social God has been generous in calling the world into being through the Word who brings life and light to the world's darkness (1:1–5); to those who receive him and believe in him he gives power to become children of God (1:12–13). The Word is the Son in the divine Family who is in the bosom of the Father and who through divine generosity becomes flesh, makes his home in the world and, full of grace, truth, and glory, makes the Father known (1:14–18). Accordingly, the fourth Gospel gives evidence through the witness of Jesus and the evangelist that the inner relationships of the social God are characterized by interpersonal communion, hospitality, and unity on the ultimate divine level, and are displayed in creation and redemption on the derivative level of nature and world history.

The principle of servanthood which Jesus enunciates to his followers in the Synoptic and Johannine accounts of his teaching—"If any one would be first, he must be last of all

121

and servant of all" (Mark 9:35b; cf. 8:35; Matt. 10:39; 16:25; Luke 9:24; 17:33; John 12:24–26)—is the principle which he implies derives from the interpersonal fidelity and hospitality of each of the three persons of the Triune Family to one another. The Father glorifies the Son and makes himself available to him, the Son glorifies the Father and defers to him, and the Holy Spirit seems almost to make himself anonymous in serving Father and Son, while they in turn appear to refer to the Spirit with loving equality and deference by sending him to carry on the work of the divine Family. Inwardly in interpersonal communion and outwardly in redemptive servanthood for the world the Triune Community exemplifies loving availability and servanthood, each for the other. The identity of Father, Son, and Holy Spirit is seen to lie in the merging of personality in interpersonal communion. There is no claim to independent individuality (which would be tritheism), but an assertion of essential identification in loving communion. On this pattern of personality in the Triune Community, Jesus prays the Father that the new society of believers may be one as the Triune Family is one. Servanthood and generosity are the key to life in the divine Community.

"All Mine Are Thine, and Thine Are Mine, and I Am Glorified in Them"
Chapter 17

It is in the prayer of Jesus in this chapter that the intimate interworking of Father and Son is most clearly expressed. The revelatory discourse has narrowed down to two persons of the divine Community, as Jesus looks back upon his faithful ministry as servant and forward to the ministry of the emerging community of believers, with the suffering of the cross now imminent. Typically, and paradoxically, he thinks of his coming glory and power, but only interpersonally as something to be shared with the Father, as together they give the gift of eternal life to the new community. Jesus can think of himself in personal terms because he consciously and voluntarily merges his will with the Father's and because he chooses to be at the disposal of the faithful. In verse 1 the mutual glorification, oneness, and equality of Father and Son are expressed in terms of mutual generosity, while verse 2 describes how the hospitality of the divine Family extends to the family of believers. The theme of reciprocal equality and sovereignty of Father and Son is interlaced with a typically selfless generosity on the part of the Son toward the Father and the world. Jesus is both Son and servant who embodies in his person the high and the low of the divine Community, both sovereign glory and servant hospitality:

17:1   "Father, the hour has come;
        glorify thy Son
        that the Son may glorify thee,
17:2   since thou hast given him
        power over all flesh,
        to give eternal life to all
            whom thou hast given him."

Repeatedly in this chapter Jesus prays the paradoxical prayer of sovereign equality with the Father which at the same time entails his conscious and willing service to the Father and his disposability on behalf of the new community. Jesus displays a consciousness of sharing in the preexistent glory of the Father and of glorifying him through his servant ministry on earth. From the standpoint of the believing community, the two aspects of Jesus' sovereign-servant status are bound together with the gift of eternal life. For believers to know Jesus Christ is to know God and to experience eternal life:

17:3   "And this is eternal life,
        that they know thee
         the only true God,
         and Jesus Christ whom thou hast sent."

As the servant Son is at the disposal of the Father and of the world, Jesus claims absolute fidelity to the Father's will and to the completion of the redemptive work he has been given to do, and accordingly is qualified to claim that he has glorified the Father in his earthly work:

123

17:4 "I glorified thee on earth,
    having accomplished the work
      which thou gavest me to do."

Conscious of his role as servant in his incarnational descent into the world, Jesus claims a mutual right to glorification with the Father in light of both his accomplished work as servant and his equality of glory with the Father before the creation of the world. Jesus displays again his consciousness of preexistence and correlativity with the Father (cf. 8:58) and prays for restoration of his glorious status in the divine ascent that follows the divine descent and shapes the U of divine disposability (cf. Phil. 2:5–11):

17:5 "And now, Father, glorify thou me in thy own
    presence
      with the glory which I had with thee
      before the world was made."

Jesus' faithful and generous servanthood on behalf of the Father and the world is couched in words of deference to the Father, for as a faithful Son he acknowledges that all believers in the new community come sovereignly from the Father; these are shared with the Son through the generosity and deference of the Father, and they in turn have kept the Father's word, thus making the circle of communion and community complete. The verbs of voluntary decision and disposability are noteworthy, as Son serves Father and believers, Father gives to believers and Son, and believers keep the word that is both Father's and Son's:

17:6 "I have manifested thy name
    to the men whom thou gavest me out of the
      world;
    thine they were,
    and thou gavest them to me,
      and they have kept thy word.

17:7 Now they know
    that everything that thou hast given me
      is from thee;

17:8   for I have given them the words
      which thou gavest me,
  and they have received them
      and know in truth that I came from thee;
  and they have believed
      that thou didst send me."

The sovereign privilege of the Father in fashioning the extended family of believers is affirmed by Jesus in his prayer for those whom the Father has given him. As Jesus defers to the Father's sovereignty, he also claims equality of possession and glorification with the Father. Thus Jesus continues to fulfill the dual role of submitted servant and sovereign Son who merges his will and possessions with the Father's, as the Father merges his will and possessions with the Son's in the creation of the new society. His immediate prayer is for the nucleus of disciples; shortly his prayer will be on behalf of those in the world to whom the disciples will minister his word (17:18–21):

17:9   "I am praying for them;
  I am not praying for the world
      but for those whom thou hast given me,
      for they are thine;
17:10   all mine are thine,
  and thine are mine,
      and I am glorified in them."

As his prayer for the disciples continues Jesus speaks of leaving the world and returning to the Father; his thought is not only of his imminent glorification but also of the welfare of the nucleus of the new community, that the Father may keep them in his name and that they may experience oneness as Son and Father experience oneness. The plurality and unity of the persons of the divine Community become the pattern of the new community of believers. Jesus fervently prays for the vindication of the social model in the new society, just as it is a reality in the Triune Family. The reality of distinct personalities within essential unity is attested in the formula "we . . . one," and is to be replicated in the circle of the redeemed "they . . . one":

17:11　"And now I am no more in the world,
　　　　　but they are in the world,
　　　　　　and I am coming to thee.
　　　　Holy Father,
　　　　　keep them in thy name
　　　　　which thou hast given me,
　　　　　　that they may be one,
　　　　　　even as we are one."

As he prays the Father to carry on his work of keeping (lit., maintaining, *tēreō*) the disciples, Jesus reviews his faithfulness in being at the disposal of his followers, so that none has been lost except Judas. In his prayer of concern for them, he amplifies the theme of verse 9 that not all the world belongs to the new society of God but only those who are kept and guarded by the Family of God. Thus Jesus claims divine sovereignty with the Father in the unfolding plan of salvation. While the focus of 14:12–19 is upon the safety and sanctification of the emerging community which is beginning to image the divine Community in its plurality and oneness, it is the generous concern of Jesus before the Father on their behalf that captures one's attention and intimates the interpersonal communion and hospitality of Son and Father as they make themselves available to one another and give themselves in unity of servanthood to the otherwise lost of the world, that the latter may have fullness of joy in their struggle with the evil one:

17:12　"While I was with them,
　　　　　I kept them in thy name,
　　　　　　which thou hast given me;
　　　　　I have guarded them,
　　　　　　and none of them is lost but the son of
　　　　　　　perdition,
　　　　　　that the scripture might be fulfilled.

17:13　But now I am coming to thee;
　　　　　and these things I speak in the world,
　　　　　　that they may have my joy fulfilled in
　　　　themselves.

17:14　I have given them thy word;
　　　　　and the world has hated them
　　　　　　because they are not of the world,
　　　　　　even as I am not of the world.

17:15 I do not pray that thou shouldst take them out of
the world,
but that thou shouldst keep them from the evil
one."

Because the disciples of the new community are not of the
world but have been transposed to the reality of the higher
Family circle, their ministry is to reflect the generous love of
the divine Community in service of others who are yet to
come into the new society. Jesus prays that they will be
sanctified in the truth of this hospitable word of grace, and
in that spirit sends them forth as he has been sent forth into
the world to minister as servant. Jesus' prayer reflects his
example and instruction in the footwashing parable of
chapter 13, as the generous Son passes on the generosity of
the Father who has sent him. The disciples of the new society are to go generously into the world with the same hospitality that motivated the Father to send the Son, and the
Son to send the disciples. This progression of love reveals
the inner relationship of the divine Community as selfless
hospitality to the other: Father and Son are utterly at the
disposal of one another in selfless and dynamic love, and
manifest this generosity to the new society, which in turn is
empowered to pass it on to others. It is to this truth of divine
disposability in loving hospitality that Jesus has consecrated
(or sanctified, *hagiazō*) himself to them, that they also may
be consecrated (or sanctified):

17:16 "They are not of the world,
even as I am not of the world.
17:17 Sanctify them in the truth;
thy word is truth.
17:18 As thou didst send me into the world,
so I have sent them into the world.
17:19 And for their sake I consecrate myself,
that they also may be consecrated in truth."

Jesus' prayer intimates that the new community subsists
by receiving and giving. Having received, believers are to
give to one another and to those who are yet to come into
fellowship through belief in Jesus. Their principal hospital-

ity to others is extended through their word of witness to the message of Jesus, which embodies the dynamic and inexhaustible love of the divine Community. It is the generous word of the believing community that bears the image of the generous Son, the result of which is unity in plurality. As the divine Community is comprised of a plurality of persons in essential unity, so the effect of preaching and belief in Jesus is the unity of believers in the Family circle:

17:20   "I do not pray for these only,
         but also for those who believe in me
            through their word,
17:21   that they may all be one;
         even as thou, Father, art in me,
         and I in thee,
     that they also may be in us,
        so that the world may believe
          that thou hast sent me."

In this prayer Jesus asks the Father that believers may participate in the divine life itself and experience unity by dwelling within the divine Community. The generosity of his prayer does not suggest an absorption into God where personality is lost, nor does it suggest that believers become a necessary and essential part of the divine Community. What it does intimate is a divine hospitality so generous that it images its own unity and interpersonal communion in the new society, and invites believers to share in its inner life. It is this unity in interpersonal fellowship that bears witness to the world and invites its belief that the Father has sent the Son. The generous prayer of Jesus intensifies as he speaks of the depth of divine hospitality in sharing with the believing community the glory which the Father has given him. The way of the higher Family is to share what is received, so that there is perfect oneness in love. As (*kathōs*) the persons of the divine Family are one, so, Jesus prays, may the believing family become perfectly one. This is the highest witness of divine love and hospitality and disposability to the world. Jesus declares that believers are loved as the Father loves the Son: as the Father is totally at the disposal of the Son in loving generosity, so the Son is totally at the disposal of believers in loving hospitality. Jesus' prayer reveals that the goal of the divine Family is to bring the separated and fallen into a redeemed and unified family that reflects the relationship of the divine persons in their ultimate oneness:

17:22 "The glory which thou hast given me
    I have given to them,
      that they may be one
      even as we are one,
17:23 I in them and thou in me,
    that they may become perfectly one,
      so that the world may know
        that thou hast sent me
        and hast loved them
        even as thou hast loved me."

Moreover, Jesus prays that the community of believers may be transposed to the higher realm that precedes and transcends the present world, to be at home with him and to behold his preexistent glory that flows from the love of the Father. It is a prayer of ascent and traces the return back to the eternal and unlimited realm of glory and grace, to the hospitality of the highest Community; for divine generosity abounds in the Father's gift of believers to the Son, in the Son's desire to share his home and his glory with the new community, and in his recognition that his glory is an eternal gift of the Father's love before the world ever was. Jesus speaks in the language of glory (*doxa*) which provides a clue to the nature of the love and glory realm that is superimposed upon this ordinary world. Jesus is in the world as incarnate Son as he prays this prayer and moves toward the fulfillment of the redemption work of the divine Family, yet he is also in another and more original world ("where I am," he says) in which the patterns of time and space are taken up into the original and are seen to be images of the glory love that eternally is and was "before the foundations of the world." The hospitality and generosity of Father and Son in

129

placing themselves at the disposal of believers and inviting them into this higher and more original glory sphere of love is characteristic of the divine life itself, for Father and Son (and Spirit) are eternally and consummately hospitable to one another in perfect unity. Both levels of hospitality and disposability are evident in Jesus' prayer:

17:24   "Father,
I desire that they also,
whom thou hast given me,
may be with me where I am,
to behold my glory
which thou hast given me
in thy love for me
before the foundation of the world."

Jesus' prayer concludes with a contrast of the unbelieving world and the community of believers. The intimate knowledge Jesus has of the Father he shares with his own who know that the Father has sent the Son. But the unknowing world (*kosmos*) has rejected its proper home in Father and Son whose "knowing" is the center of the new society; and so for the unbelieving world there is, by implication, no possibility of real and lasting community apart from the Community of God. In the final refrain of his prayer Jesus acclaims once more the likeness of the Father's love for believers and his love for the Son, the equality of Father and Son, and the inexhaustible and dynamic love of the divine Community for the redeemed community as divine knowledge and love are to be poured out in mutual indwelling and interpersonal communion:

17:25   "O righteous Father,
the world has not known thee,
but I have known thee;
'and these know that thou hast sent me.
17:26   I made known to them thy name,
and I will make it known,
that the love with which thou hast loved me
may be in them,
and I in them."

Jesus' high-priestly prayer to the Father discloses the social nature of the divine Family. It underscores Jesus' teaching throughout his ministry that God is social and that creation, insofar as it images God, is also social in nature. Individuality is real, as are Father, Son, and Holy Spirit; however, true individuality is not separateness or egocentricity but faithful interrelatedness in oneness. As with believers in the new community, so with the divine Community in the highest and most original sense: reality lies in generous love and being at one another's disposal. As he faces his final act of disposability, Jesus proclaims in intercessory prayer that this is the highest and final glory for God as well as believers.

The Community of God
and the Dominion of Darkness
Chapters 18–19

The intimate communion of the divine Family and its hospitality to the believing community continues to make itself evident as the drama of Jesus' passion unfolds. When he is arrested in the garden and Peter tries to defend him by the sword, Jesus rebukes Peter for placing the sword before the cup of suffering which the Son must drink. The sword represents the way of the world, the cup the way of the Family of God, for the Father has given his Son for the salvation of the world to drink the cup of divine wrath against sin and rebellion (Ps. 75:8; Isa. 51:17, 22; Jer. 13:12–14; 25:15–16), and the Son wills to be obedient to the Father's call. Jesus' response explicitly affirms his desire to be at the disposal of the Father; implicitly it acclaims the generous disposability of the divine Family, acting as one on behalf of the new community that is being called out of the world:

18:11   Jesus said to Peter,
        "Put your sword into its sheath;
        shall I not drink the cup
            which the Father has given me?"

131

The emerging new community is not itself ready to drink the cup of suffering hospitality. Jesus is increasingly deserted by his followers and finally stands alone as the representative of divine disposability. The contrast of unfaithfulness and faithfulness is ironically described in Peter's denial of Jesus at the moment when Jesus is standing before Annas and Caiaphas and shortly thereafter before Pilate in faithful testimony to the reality of the kingdom community that is not of this world (18:36). Jesus voices the social aims of the divine Community, but not in terms of the fallen world order and selfish political ambition. In view of the total scene described in chapter 18, the irony of contrasts centers on the one hand upon Peter and Pilate, two disparate individuals who desperately want to be accepted on pragmatic and temporal terms that will secure them immediate release from pain without regard for long-term consequences; and Jesus on the other hand who is ready to suffer immediate pain and separation from worldly security in order to secure the long-term consequences of his social kingship. Jesus declares in effect that the family of believers he is creating as the incarnate spokesman of the divine Family is from above and not from below. True community for those below can come only from the Community above. When Pilate cynically dismisses Judaism and reminds Jesus that his own nation has repudiated him (18:35), Jesus responds by claiming a higher kind of authority and society:

18:36   "My kingship is not of this world;
            if my kingship were of this world,
                my servants would fight,
                that I might not be handed over to the Jews;
            but my kingship is not from the world."

Pilate's rhetorical question, "So you are a king?" (18:37a), receives no further clarification from Jesus except what may be discerned by those who hear his voice and understand the truth of who he is and what he is doing.

18:37   "You say that I am a king.
            For this I was born,

> and for this I have come into the world,
>   to bear witness to the truth.
> Every one who is of the truth
>   hears my voice."

For those who hear his voice and discern the truth, Jesus is indeed King of the new society. But Pilate's cynical reply, "What is truth?" (v. 38), indicates that he neither hears nor discerns the truth of Jesus' person and his social mission. Although he personally finds no crime in Jesus (18:38; 19:6), he lacks the integrity to make a just political decision because he is a self-seeking questioner without ethical absolutes or a genuine sense of community. In terms of their own tradition and pragmatic concern for immediate national security, the religious authorities view Jesus as a threat; by his claim to membership in the divine Family as self-proclaimed Son of God they consider him guilty of blasphemy, and call upon Pilate to put him to death:

19:7   "We have a law, and by that law
        he ought to die,
    because he has made himself
        the Son of God."

Pilate finds his own security threatened by this request ("When Pilate heard these words, he was the more afraid" [v. 8]) and resumes his questioning of Jesus, flaunting his belief that he has political power to release him or to crucify him, in an attempt to get him to answer his inquiry (v. 10). Jesus' bold rebuttal of the civil authority who is to order him crucified confirms his confident assurance that he is one with the divine Community "from above" that is sovereign over the affairs of history:

19:11   Jesus answered him,
        "You would have no power over me
            unless it had been given you from above."

In this brief reply Jesus claims the transcendent power of the sovereign Family that is redemptively at work in the world and is holding worldly leadership responsible for its exercise of delegated power. Caiaphas the high priest is most responsible as the highest representative of the messianic tradition because he has defaulted as the keeper of God's community and has become its bitterest enemy in rejecting the Son of the divine Community and delivering him up to be crucified: "therefore he who has delivered me to you has the greater sin" (v. 11b). The irony of the trial is heightened by the fact that the chief enemies of the redemptive hospitality of the Family of God embodied in Jesus the Son are the supposed guardians of Israel's prophetic tradition concerning the new community of the messianic age (19:12–16; cf. 18:12–24). It is they who call opportunistically for the crucifixion of the King and idolatrously swear allegiance to Caesar alone ("We have no king but Caesar" [v. 15]).

This final rejection of the King of the new community for immediate worldly security takes place against the backdrop of the Passover feast which Jesus is bringing to fulfillment in his death and resurrection. The common theme of Passover and the cross focuses upon divine disposability on behalf of a sinful world. The final and redeeming irony of the trial is that inadvertently both secular and religious factions, aiming at disposing of the disposable King, actually create the conditions by which the rejected Son and King of the divine Community brings the new society into being. Jesus affirms that God is sovereign over historical events and weaves even the most extreme rejection of divine hospitality into a compound good. The new society of God is about to emerge in power; the secular and religious powers that now hold sway are under divine judgment and will wane. Both Pilate and Caiaphas and their respective communities exercise their oppressive power only by divine permission, and both are doomed because of their rejection of the true community, Caiaphas committing the greater sin because he is keeper of the messianic tradition.

Ironically the reality of Jesus' kingship finds final verbal expression in the title placed on the cross as Pilate and Caiaphas's circle of chief priests vie over the exact wording, Pilate out of contempt for the Jewish tradition insisting on

"Jesus of Nazareth, the King of the Jews," the chief priests out of disdain for Jesus and his community insisting on "This man said, I am King of the Jews" (19:19–21). The concluding irony is that the secular cynicism of Pilate has the final word and speaks the greater truth ("What I have written I have written" [v. 22]), not the final redaction of the spokesmen of the messianic heritage. The title stands, the evangelist infers, as the true statement of the crucifixion. Seen from above through the eyes of belief, the cross is the point at which the hostile world seems to triumph in disposing of Jesus the King, when in fact it is where Jesus the King makes himself utterly disposable in divine hospitality and becomes the seed of the new society (12:24).

Jesus' sensitivity to the smaller circles of family in his hour of anguish is reflected in his concern for his mother, as he directs her and the beloved disciple to be as mother and son to each other ("Woman, behold your son!"; "Behold, your mother" [19:26–27]). This seemingly incidental vignette portrays a small detail on the larger canvas of the divine disposability Jesus embodies in his person on the cross. Although he is about to accomplish the work that will make the larger redeemed family a reality, Jesus displays in his final moment of suffering a tenderness close and small that will provide a pattern for believers in their relationships within the new family. According to the account, the beloved disciple is obedient to his Lord's request and places himself at the disposal of Mary, in imitation of Jesus' hospitality ("And from that hour the disciple took her to his own home" [v. 27b]).

The irony of Jesus' crucifixion in the context of the Passover feast comes to final expression as he anguishes in thirst in his true humanity, receives the vinegar offered him, and speaks his final word as the Word become flesh: "It is finished" (*tetelestai*). This verb of completion brings to a triumphant close the quest of the incarnate Logos (1:14) who enters upon his hospitable mission of salvation to form a new community in the image of his own divine Community. The Gospel of John is summarized in the final *tetelestai* of Jesus the Son who is King of a new kingdom that ironically brings

135

eternal life as he is lifted up on the cross and dies (cf. 3:3, 5, 14–16).

It is noteworthy that the evangelist in his selection and arrangement of materials has introduced Nicodemus early on, together with Jesus' equation of the kingdom of God and eternal life (3:1–15). The essential themes of Jesus' mission are given there, including his prophecy of being lifted up, and are reiterated as they come to fulfillment in the trial and crucifixion near the end of the Gospel. It is not until the trial that Jesus speaks again of his kingship and is called king (18:33–37; 19:14–22), and it is not until after Jesus' death on the cross that Nicodemus appears again, with Joseph of Arimathea, to take away the body of Jesus for burial (19:38–42). Thus the early themes of the seeking Nicodemus and the lifting up of Jesus are brought to climax in the crucifixion of Jesus and the faithful discipleship of Nicodemus. Earlier Jesus has spoken to Nicodemus of the kingdom of God and eternal life; now Nicodemus wraps the body of the dead King in linen and spices and lays him in a tomb. Irony and faith are stretched near to breaking, for the promise of eternal life in a new community appears to have died with the disposal of the body of Jesus in a tomb. But the resolution comes in the sequel.

"Blessed Are Those Who Have Not Seen and Yet Believe"
Chapter 20

Unlikely persons appear in the narrative following Jesus' crucifixion. One would not have expected Joseph of Arimathea or Nicodemus to have come forward in faithful service and at considerable personal risk to perform the last rites of burial, but perhaps Peter or the beloved disciple, or any of the others from the inner core of disciples. Peter and "the other disciple" do examine the empty tomb when Mary Magdalene reports the fact to them (20:1–9), but the reader is surprised again to discover that the risen Jesus favors Mary with personal address, calling her by name and sending her to proclaim to the waiting circle of the new community that he is ascending to the Father. He warns her not to hold on to him possessively ("Stop clinging to me," *mē mou haptou*, v. 17), for he has not yet completed the circle of family communion by ascending to the Father. She is to place herself at his disposal and announce to the disciples his impending ascension to his Father who is also their Father God. The first missionary directive of the risen Jesus is framed within the social context of Jesus and Mary; it embraces the community of disciples and is authenticated by the divine Community of Father and Son:

20:17 "But go to my brethren and say to them,
  I am ascending to my Father
    and your Father,
  to my God
    and your God."

The authentication of the societal mission of the new community is given by Jesus on the evening of that day in the context of the gathered family of disciples. He speaks peace to them, shows them his hands and side as evidence of his identity and disposability on their behalf, and commissions them in the name of the Triune Family to go and minister forgiveness of sins as he has been sent by the Father to forgive sins (20:19–23). Jesus speaks with divine authority as he grants them peace, and at the same time defers to the Father who has sent him, calling on his disciples to defer to him as he sends them forth. The new community is to be identified by deference and servanthood, since it is the essential nature of the divine Community, as revealed by the Son, to be generous and hospitable:

20:21 "Peace be with you.
  As the Father has sent me,
    even so I send you."

The third person of the Triune Family is invoked by Jesus the Son as he prepares the witnessing community to proclaim forgiveness of sins and to carry on his finished work:

20:22 And when he had said this,
  he breathed on them, and said to them,
    "Receive the Holy Spirit."

137

Assuming his divine status and acting as God the Creator in Genesis 2:7 (where the same verb, *enephusēsen*, is used; cf. also Ezek. 37:9), Jesus the Son breathes on the new society divine life; the Holy Spirit is now in the faithful community, to be poured out in power on the day of Pentecost (Acts 2, in fulfillment of Acts 1:5, 8). John the evangelist does not describe the initial giving of the Holy Spirit in terms of individual gifts, but as a gift of the divine Family made to the family of believers as a gathered community. The divine Community is social and is reflected by the in-breathing of the Holy Spirit on the redeemed society as a unity. The collective witnessing community is given a Spirit-filled authority to proclaim forgiveness of sins to the world, the effect of which is, as in the ministry of Jesus himself, that some believe and become members of the community and others do not (the likely meaning of v. 23; the text does not mean that special individuals in the community are empowered to grant or withhold forgiveness).

The incident of Thomas's doubting and Jesus' rebuke of his demand for hard facts illustrates the importance of belief in entering the family of God (20:24–29). Thomas comes to confession of faith when he actually sees and touches the risen body of Jesus and receives the compassionate rebuke, "Do not be faithless, but believing." Sight opens the way to belief in Jesus' lordship and deity ("My Lord and my God!" v. 28). But Jesus rebukes this attitude and declares that access to life in the community of God comes not by evidence on demand, where the Lord is put on trial, but by placing oneself at the disposal of Jesus in faithful belief and service, whether one sees clearly or not:

20:29   Jesus said to him,
      "Have you believed because you have seen me?
      Blessed are those who have not seen
      and yet believe."

To this the evangelist adds his justification for writing the Gospel. Entrance into the family of God is through belief in Jesus the Messiah, the Son of God; in his name is life, and life, according to Jesus, is fellowship in the community of the kingdom of God. John's purpose in writing the Gospel is that believers may be strengthened and new believers may enter God's new society:

20:31   But these are written that you may believe
                    that Jesus is the Christ,
                    the Son of God,
             and that believing
                    you may have life in his name.

"Feed My Sheep"
Chapter 21

The concluding appearance of Jesus to his disciples by the Sea of Tiberias (21:1–23) is the epilogue of John's portrait of Jesus and the community he is bringing into being. (The authenticity of this chapter is debated in critical circles, but forms a coherent unity with the main text of the Gospel.) The disciples are discouraged at having caught nothing through the night, but Jesus confidently appears at break of day and guides them to a miraculous catch of fish (vv. 1–8). This is probably an acted parable that anticipates the generosity of the risen Christ in the coming mission of his followers who will become fishers of men (cf. Mark 1:17 para.). Jesus exercises divine power in a generous manner as Lord of nature in order to feed his disciples with temporal and physical food, as he invites them to share in a common breakfast of bread and fish, over which he officiates (vv. 9–14). In view of all that Jesus has previously taught in word and deed concerning himself as life-giving food and as servant of divine disposability, obedience, and mission (e.g., 6:1–14, 25–59; 12:24–26; 13:12–20), it is likely that he is further instructing his community of disciples in faithfulness to his commands and generous hospitality, and is drawing them away from fruitless despondency to fruitful disposability on behalf of those for whom he has died and risen.

Jesus' conversation with Peter (21:15–19) is intended to convey to the social unity of the disciples his challenge and commission to feed and tend his sheep. As Peter is reinstated by thrice affirming his love for Jesus, thus redeeming his three denials during the trial, so Jesus invites the new community in his appeal to Peter to feed his lambs and tend and feed his sheep. Through the person of the risen Son who speaks for the divine Community, the new society of disciples is commissioned to carry on his work of hospitality and disposability for those who do come into the family of God.

The fourth Gospel concludes, accordingly, on a note of divine generosity. To be at the disposal of others may entail personal sacrifice of life (21:18–19), as Jesus gave up his life for the world. Divine hospitality requires that the new society be ready to obey the final word of invitation from the Son of the divine Society—"Follow me" (21:19, 22). Following Jesus the incarnate Son leads homeward to eternal life in fellowship with the Triune Community (14:1–3, 23). This, John tells us, is why he wrote his Gospel (20:31), for it is the Gospel of homecoming.

Appendix
The Historicity, Date, and Authorship of the Fourth Gospel

D. Moody Smith, in a recent review of Ernst Haenchen, *Das Johannesevangelium: Ein Kommentar* (Tübingen: Mohr [Siebeck], 1980), makes an astute and compelling observation regarding the limitations of the critical method in reconstructing the historical setting of the fourth Gospel. He writes (*Journal of Biblical Literature*, vol. 102 [June 1983]: 348):

> We are trained to interpret texts so as to get at the meaning which an author whom we do not know, who lived 2,000 years ago, intended for an audience we do not know! That is risky business at best. It becomes even more risky when several hypothetical authors are involved. Is there a possibility of interpreting a text, not ahistorically, but with reference to the realities to which the text points and irrespective of whether that text has one or more authors? This is not a suggestion that historical and literary, or source and redaction, criticism be abandoned, but that they be qualified as hermeneutical tools. Perhaps a move in the direction of consolidating Johannine interpretation, although still within the framework and presuppositions of conventional N[ew] T[estament] criticism, is Hartwig Thyen's decision to regard the redactor, who after all gave the Gospel of John its final framework, as the evangelist (as is the case in synoptic criticism) and to proceed exegetically on that basis: that is, to interpret the gospel from the standpoint of that redaction.

While I share neither Smith's concurrence with Haenchen that the material in John is "more often than not historically inferior to what we find in the Synoptics" (p. 347), nor his agnosticism that often the text is not historical at all, I do agree that it is important to approach the Gospel as a finished whole and to exegete the text as it stands in its final form. This I have tried to do in a descriptive (or phenomenological) manner, exegeting the passages that have to do directly or indirectly with Jesus' relationship to the Father and to the Holy Spirit. Those who doubt the historicity of much of the fourth Gospel, especially the high christological passages in which Jesus consciously claims equality with the Father, are of course faced with the question of the value of such texts, other than as evidence of an earlier faith and as objects for critical reflection. If the language of Jesus in the Gospel tells us little that is ontologically true about Jesus' understanding of himself and of the essential social relationship of Father, Son, and Spirit, then the religious value of the Gospel of John becomes an undefined and subjective matter for the individual interpreter, and has little to do with the claims of the evangelist that he is authentically describing the nature of God in terms of the Son's incarnate and historical disclosure of the divine intention.

On the other hand, if the interpreter accepts John's portrait of Jesus as authentic and reliable because it comes from the hand of a fellow believer who was an eyewitness and was inspired of the Holy Spirit to give reliable historical data, not pious fiction, then the fourth Gospel is a source of valuable information regarding the social nature of God the Triune Community. I have taken the second approach (either is a presupposition that governs the use of the tools of exegesis), not only because I stand existentially within the community of faith that accepts the witness of the gospel writers as historically reliable, but because I am convinced intellectually that a better case can be made exegetically of the data when a positive presupposition rather than a negative presupposition governs the tools of research.

In view of the fact that the reconstruction of the setting and the meaning of the fourth Gospel is, according to Smith, "risky business at best," especially when it is assumed that critics really do not know the original author(s) or audience, it would be best to begin by being truly "scientific" in the broadest phenomenological sense and simply describe what is going on in the Gospel as it stands, that is, what the claims of Jesus are, and what the supportive claims of the evangelist appear to be. When we do this, several important

142

claims appear to be foremost in the mind of the evangelist. First, he asserts the historical reality of the incarnation ("And the Word became flesh and dwelt among us, full of grace and truth"), and that the glory of this remarkable Person was beheld by eyewitnesses, of whom he is one ("we have beheld his glory, glory as of the only Son from the Father" [1:14]). Second, he selects from the treasury of sayings and acts of Jesus remembrances that empirically evidence Jesus' authoritative teaching and ministry and support the claim of 1:14.

Third, the evangelist avers that the historical truth and meaning of the incarnate Son of God are attested, according to the testimony of Jesus himself, by the activity of the Holy Spirit ("But the Counselor, the Holy Spirit, whom the Father will send in my name, he will teach you all things, and bring to your remembrance all that I have said to you" [14:26]); hence the author is confident that what he has written in his Gospel is historically true and reliable because the Holy Spirit, together with the Father, bears witness to the Son (see 15:26). Fourth, the evangelist is so convinced of the truth claims of Jesus and is so confident of his own faith that he writes his Gospel with the express purpose of convincing others to believe and to experience life in Christ ("but these are written that you may believe that Jesus is the Christ, the Son of God, and that believing you may have life in his name" [20:31]).

Accordingly, it is clear from a simple description of key themes in the Gospel that the intention of the evangelist is to present trustworthy testimony regarding the incarnate Son of God, of whom he claims to be an eyewitness, and that the reliability of his witness is underwritten, in his estimation, by the Holy Spirit. At this point the exegete must make a decision either to accept the testimony or to question it. To question it is "risky business" because the interpreter is then thrown upon his own imaginative resources to reconstruct hypothetically what he thinks actually happened. This is not necessarily more scientific, although it does open the door to unlimited artistic imagination on the part of the historiographer, who is now free to test every hypothesis except the one advanced by the evangelist himself. At the same time the

143

interpreter has to trust the evangelist to some unspecified degree that is again subjective, since most of the data that are to be used for reconstruction come perforce from the hand of the evangelist.

The dating of the fourth Gospel is related to the larger question of the origin of the Gospels as a whole, and this again is "risky business." Although the most widely accepted hypothesis places the Gospel of Mark first as the earliest of the Gospels, completed perhaps around A.D. 68 (Matthew and Luke likely following in the 80s, redacting Mark and using perhaps a hypothetical Q sayings source as well as special M and special L respectively, John following last in the 90s as a unique specimen of the gospel genre), many, including myself, are less than happy about this imaginative reconstruction. For those trained in text criticism, who tend to take the shorter reading as the more original and authentic, it seems to make sense to take the shorter Mark as the original which Matthew and Luke use extensively, since so much common material is found in all three. There is no doubt that a careful line-by-line comparison of the Synoptics in parallel does indicate some source that is common to all three, while John is either unaware of or intentionally complementary to the synoptic tradition. On the other hand, placing Mark close to the date of the fall of Jerusalem forces Matthew, Luke, and John to follow in succession like a train following an engine, so that no one of the four, being beyond the epoch of the living eyewitness apostles, can claim apostolic authorship in its final form. This relatively late and lengthy period also gives the interpreter occasion to explain the evolution of doctrine in the church and the trajectory of a high Christology that finds its culmination in the fourth Gospel in the 90s.

Most gospel studies are based on this hypothesis and, in the present era of research, appear mainly concerned to show the distinctive redactional or creative theologies of the individual evangelists who reflect a diversity of belief in the widely separated centers of Christian faith in the fourth quarter of the first century. This configuration of events has favored a general agnosticism regarding the historicity of the sayings and acts ascribed to Jesus in the Gospels, especially Jesus' messianic claims and intimations of oneness with the Father. In view of the latter, the historicity of the "high" sayings of Jesus in the Gospel of John is highly suspect because it is thought that its final redactor(s) have placed on the lips of Jesus sayings of pious fiction that have been filtered through the medium of faith and were never intended to be taken as historical fact: thus Rudolf Schnackenburg, who asserts, "In the case of the fourth evangelist, it was clearly not his intention to offer his readers a purely historical chronicle of events . . . We must perceive the eternal message which the Gospel wishes to bring us."[1]

But certainly this presupposition regarding the intention of the evangelist must be considered docetic and gnostic if it implies a reticence to believe that a historical person like Jesus could have uttered such high theological declamations. We would thus look for the "eternal message" that transcends the historical (whatever that might be), rather than the eternal God speaking and acting through the incarnate Son, Jesus. If it were the case, however, that the author(s) of the Gospel did indeed intend to write in docetic fashion, employing a high Christology but only of the risen Christ, not of the historical Jesus, then the incarnational theme of 1:14 would have to be taken as an afterthought, even though it appears programmatically in the prologue. The sayings of Jesus would accordingly reside in the sphere of religious experience or gnosis, not in the arena of history. They would be either sayings of the risen Christ given by divine inspiration to the evangelist(s) of what Jesus might have said but did not say, or piously imaginative creations of the evangelist(s) and the community. Thus the high Christology of the fourth Gospel would indicate its lateness in the evolutionary development of gospel traditions.

The presupposition that a high Christology is late does not withstand careful scrutiny, however, when one realizes that the equally high Christology of Paul can be dated from the late 40s, if Galatians is placed early, and certainly from the decade of the 50s when most of the Pauline epistles were

---

1. Rudolf Schnackenburg, *The Gospel According to Saint John*, trans. Kevin Smyth, 3 vols. (New York: Seabury, 1979), vol. 1, p. 25.

written. On the christological level there is no reason why the Gospels could not have been written in their present form during the theologically fertile decade of the 50s, or at least by the early 60s in the case of John.

It may be that the Gospels were written in stages by their authors, in which case the dates of formative composition are actually much earlier, going back to written as well as oral eyewitness reports as early as the 30s and 40s, when a highly verbal and articulate kerygmatic church would preserve for proclamation, worship, and instruction a written body of material to be drawn on as the mission of the church quickly expanded from the epicenter of Jerusalem. The allusions in the Gospels to persecution and conflict with synagogue can more easily be explained as descriptive of Jesus' own setting and the early period following than to imagine that later redactors have superimposed their own post-70 situations of persecution and conflict with synagogue upon the material and contemporized Jesus to speak as the risen Christ to their specific situations. If that were the case, we would be hard pressed to explain why in the Gospels nothing other than general prophecies before the event is made of the climactic destruction of the temple in Jerusalem, the decisive event that phases out the locus of ritual sacrifice for Judaism and obviates the Jewish-Christian question, since the central focus of traditional ritualism has been eliminated.

For these and other reasons the precise origin of the Gospels must, in this world at least, remain an open question, other than the Gospels' own attestation to their historicity. There is no way of determining with precision which of the synoptic Gospels came first, or whether they all sprang up concurrently, drawing upon a large body of oral and written material that would account for verbal similarities as well as complementary aspections of Jesus' acts and sayings. Sometimes we think we can detect the hand of the evangelist in selecting this or omitting that, but we can make serious mistakes if we forget that an intinerant preacher like Jesus over a period of three or more years would have proclaimed common themes in a variety of patterns; hence we do not even know in many instances where the Gospels are arranged in parallel columns whether we have a single original that is paraphrased by the other evangelists, or a genuinely different saying uttered on a separate occasion, in which case the versions are not parallel and should not so appear without a caveat. (For additional perspectives on the question, see Robert W. Funk, *New Gospel Parallels*, vol. 1 [Philadelphia: Fortress, 1985], and Joseph B. Tyson and Thomas R. W. Longstaff, *Synoptic Abstract* in *The Computer Bible*, vol. 15 [Wooster, Ohio: Biblical Research Associates, 1978]).

Accordingly the interpreter must be wary in using a gospel-parallels version when doing exegesis, and must bear in mind that the parallel columns arranged by the editor may not reflect the redactional activity of the evangelists at all, but rather Jesus' own variety of expression of a common theme on different occasions. One would not want to repeat the mistakes of former Old Testament interpreters of the Pentateuch and assume that blue, red, and green underlinings of parallel columns tell us very much about the way the Gospels were necessarily written, or who borrowed from whom and redacted more extravangantly. It is very "risky business."

We may assume that there was a common core of sayings and acts of Jesus that lay behind the Gospels, but how it came to be shaped into the present forms of the Gospels themselves is largely beyond our ken. I am personally skeptical about linear models, whether Markan or Matthaean or Lukan, because they tend to be too simplistic and encourage easy redactional solutions to the complex questions of gospel origins. That the gospel writers select, arrange, and sometimes paraphrase the sayings of Jesus in fashioning their Gospels goes without saying. How they do it is a hypothetical matter that allows a number of possible solutions.

What is of greater importance than the question of the priority of Mark or the priority of Matthew, or whether Matthew and Luke used hypothetical Q or Luke used Matthew as a sayings source, is the question of dating. As important as Luke's declaration of intention that he has accurately consulted eyewitness accounts (Luke 1:1–4) is the fact that volume 2 of his narrative, the Book of Acts, ends where it does, before the trial of Paul in Rome (28:30–31). That there is no mention of the death of James the Lord's brother in 62, nor any hint of the impending destruction of Jerusalem is significant. The most reasonable inference is that Luke finished Acts at least by 62, and the Gospel of Luke sometime earlier, perhaps as early as the mid to late 50s. If one insists on Markan priority, that is, that Luke used the finished Gospel of Mark in compiling his own Gospel, then Mark must also be dated no later than the early 60s. It follows that the Gospel of Matthew need not be placed in the shadowy depository of the 80s but could also have been written in the same general frame of time—unless, of course, Matthew is the first Gospel, in which case it could be still earlier. The Gospel of John could in that case be written by an eyewitness, John the beloved disciple, who, although conversant with the synoptic narratives, chooses to write a Gospel that gives a historically trustworthy but complementary account of selected sayings and acts of Jesus. In that case the date of the fourth Gospel would be slightly later than the Synoptics but certainly before the destruction of Jerusalem, as it makes no allusions to that cataclysmic event, and in fact describes conditions that actually obtained before 70.

There is an even more important question than that of dating, however, and it is the crucial element in what will always be a circular argument in regard to the origin of the Gospels. This is the christological question: how seriously will the historian/interpreter take the witness of the four Gospels that Jesus made remarkable claims about his messianic mission and his standing in the place of God? Presuppositions play a subtle but important role at the beginning of the critical process, for if the interpreter is predisposed to doubt that Jesus ever made, or ever could have made, such claims, then the gospel writers must have created them and placed them on Jesus' lips after the fact. If one believes that, then sufficient time is needed for a high Christology to evolve among the churches. Probably this presupposition weighs more heavily than any other factor in the late dating of the Gospels and the model of linear dependency beginning with Mark around 68 and concluding with John in the 90s. In that configuration there are no apostolic eyewitnesses writing the Gospels, and Jesus has become a shadowy figure whose "authentic" voice is difficult to hear and whose genuine sayings are minimal. The fourth Gospel must then be seen as docetic and gnostic in its high Christology, even though it may be seen to contain much else that is of historical value. But for our purposes in the present study the Gospel would not tell us much that is ontologically true about the relationship of Father, Son, and Holy Spirit as revealed by the incarnate Son, Jesus Christ, in our history.

On the other hand, if the interpreter believes that the gospel writers are fellow Christians who can be trusted because they have experienced the inner as well as the outer dimensions of the historical phenomenon of Jesus Christ, and that the Father and the Son have sent the Holy Spirit to ensure the integrity of the gospel narratives through divine inspiration, then one can exegete the text confidently, knowing that when Jesus is described as speaking or acting, he is doing so historically and as genuinely incarnate, not as a figure of minimal historical reality who has been placed in a setting of pious fiction. As that is the presupposition which I share with the evangelists (as I read their intention not to write fictionally) I find no difficulty in believing that Jesus really said and did what John the beloved disciple describes of him in his Gospel, and trusting this brother in Christ I have proceeded to exegete the sayings of Jesus as I have found them, sincerely believing that what the incarnate Son said about his relationship to the Father and the Holy Spirit informs us of the true nature of the Triune Family. This, of course, is "risky business," but then it always has been. At least it is something for which it is worth considerable risk, for it does far more justice to the logically "odd" character of the Gospel than can be accommodated by secular norms of exegesis. I. T. Ramsey catches the point well when he observes:

> The "facts" of the Gospels in particular are never facts for which science is appropriate currency, or history is appropriate currency. The paradigm is *ho logos sarx egeneto.*
>
> In all, we must recognize that the language of the Bible, and of the Gospels in particular, must be odd enough to be appropriate to the odd situations which are their subject. If then we are to resolve the philosophical difficulties which biblical criticism presents to us, we will have to gain more

insight into the peculiar *logical* structure the evangelists gave to their language when they wrote the Gospels to tell of the "wonderful works of God."[2]

In a concluding postscript, I would say that when the interpreter has settled the christological question, the dates will be found to fall more or less into place. If the Christology is "low," the dates will more than likely tend to be late; if the Christology is "high," the dates will likely be early. There are exceptions, of course. Some, like J. A. T. Robinson, whose Christology is not particularly high (see *The Human Face of God* [Philadelphia: Westminster, 1973]), argue for the pre-70 dating of all the New Testament books on internal and external arguments apart from the christological question (*Redating the New Testament* [Philadelphia: Westminster, 1976], see especially chaps. 1, 2, 4, 9, 11). Others, whose Christology appears to be traditional, opt for later dates because they are for various reasons committed to a linear model that begins with Mark in the late 60s and ends with John in the 90s. Generally, the latter group incline to greater employment of redactional methodology than I find acceptable and give evidence of kenotic and/or docetic tendencies in attributing high christological sayings in the Gospels to the "risen Christ" (speaking to Christian prophets like John) rather than to Jesus the incarnate Son.

The question of Jesus' personal consciousness of his role and status is therefore central to the debate over the origin of the Gospels, because it is necessary to know whether a high Christology begins with Jesus himself or is added later in the redactional evolution of church theology. If the former is true, there is no compelling reason to date the Gospels late. But even if the interpreter travels the second route, there is still no necessity to date late, because a high Christology is already present in the Pauline writings of the 50s and early 60s and could just as well appear in the Gospels during the same period.

There are, accordingly, good arguments for dating all four

2. I. T. Ramsey, *Religious Language: An Empirical Placing of Theological Phrases* (New York: Macmillan, 1963), pp. 122–23.

Gospels prior to 70, and I have mentioned several of them. Regarding the order of the appearance of the Gospels, there are any number of hypotheses that are reasonable and possible, including both Markan and Matthaean priority, granted that the dates are early enough (see, e.g., the measured and cautious discussion by D. A. Carson in his commentary on Matthew, *The Expositor's Bible Commentary,* ed. Frank E. Gaebelein, vol. 8 [Grand Rapids: Zondervan, 1984], pp. 11–21). My own analysis of the data would suggest that it is likely that the gospel writers employed a variety of eyewitness accounts, the use of some of which would account for synoptic verbal parallels, while the selection of others would account for varieties in presentation, and that the final editions of the synoptic Gospels appeared concurrently during the great fertile period of the 50s. John, I believe, would have known of the Synoptics and was led to add his own eyewitness testimony as a complementary portrait, his final edition (if indeed there were several stages of composition) appearing in the late 50s or early 60s. The written origins of all four Gospels would therefore extend backward to eyewitness accounts in the 30s and to the high christological affirmations of Jesus himself. This is all hypothetical, of course, but makes more sense of the data than competing theories and at the same time honors the integrity of the evangelists as responsible witnesses to the person of Jesus, whose spoken and acted language thus appears in the four Gospels in four reliable and complementary portraits.

With a high Christology emanating from the person of Jesus himself, in keeping with the thematic declaration of John 1:14, the stage is set for the creative use of the historical and grammatical tools of scholarship in exegeting the fourth Gospel. When these are used with respect for the integrity of the evangelist as an interpreter of the dramatic story which centers upon the incarnate Son of the Triune Community, and with a sense of gratitude for the Holy Spirit's role as guarantor of the historical truthfulness of the storyline, the interpreter may exercise discernment in weighing the insights of commentators who have examined the Gospel from many exegetical angles, without having to concur with all their interpretations or theological perspectives. This has been true of the present volume as I have interacted, among many volumes and articles, with the principal contemporary epoch-making commentaries on the fourth Gospel, including those of C. H. Dodd, *The Interpretation of the Fourth Gospel* (Cambridge: Cambridge University Press, 1953); C. K. Barrett, *Gospel According to Saint John* (London: S.P.C.K., 1955); Rudolf Bultmann, *The Gospel of John: A Commentary*, translated by G. R. Beasley-Murray, R. W. N. Hoare, and J. K. Riches (Philadelphia: Westminster, 1971), the English translation of *Das Evangelium des Johannes* (Göttingen: Vandenhoeck und Ruprecht, 1966); Raymond E. Brown, *The Gospel According to John*, vols. 29, 30, *The Anchor Bible* (Garden City, N.Y.: Doubleday, 1966); Rudolf Schnackenburg, *The Gospel According to Saint John*, translated by Kevin Smyth, 3 vols. (New York: Seabury, 1979), the English translation of *Das Johannesevangelium* (Freiburg: Herder, 1965); R. Alan Culpepper, *Anatomy of the Fourth Gospel: A Study in Literary Design* (Philadelphia: Fortress, 1983). For faithfully consistent interpreters of the Gospel from former periods, John Calvin (*Commentary on the Gospel According to John*, translated by William Pringle, 2 vols. [Grand Rapids: Eerdmans, 1949]) and B. F. Westcott (*A Commentary on the Gospel According to Saint John* [reprint ed., Grand Rapids: Eerdmans, 1950]) remain valuable friends, as does Leon Morris in the contemporary setting (*The Gospel According to John*, the New International Commentary on the New Testament series [Grand Rapids: Eerdmans, 1971]).

Subject and Author Index

Scripture Index